The Expre  .... Education

Lucy Barbera

The Expressive Arts in Teacher Education

Cultivating Social Justice Leadership

LAP LAMBERT Academic Publishing

Impressum/Imprint (nur für Deutschland/ only for Germany)

Bibliografische Information der Deutschen Nationalbibliothek: Die Deutsche Nationalbibliothek verzeichnet diese Publikation in der Deutschen Nationalbibliografie; detaillierte bibliografische Daten sind im Internet über http://dnb.d-nb.de abrufbar.

Alle in diesem Buch genannten Marken und Produktnamen unterliegen warenzeichen-, marken- oder patentrechtlichem Schutz bzw. sind Warenzeichen oder eingetragene Warenzeichen der jeweiligen Inhaber. Die Wiedergabe von Marken, Produktnamen, Gebrauchsnamen, Handelsnamen, Warenbezeichnungen u.s.w. in diesem Werk berechtigt auch ohne besondere Kennzeichnung nicht zu der Annahme, dass solche Namen im Sinne der Warenzeichen- und Markenschutzgesetzgebung als frei zu betrachten wären und daher von jedermann benutzt werden dürften.

Coverbild: www.ingimage.com

Verlag: LAP LAMBERT Academic Publishing GmbH & Co. KG
Dudweiler Landstr. 99, 66123 Saarbrücken, Deutschland
Telefon +49 681 3720-310, Telefax +49 681 3720-3109
Email: info@lap-publishing.com

Herstellung in Deutschland:
Schaltungsdienst Lange o.H.G., Berlin
Books on Demand GmbH, Norderstedt
Reha GmbH, Saarbrücken
Amazon Distribution GmbH, Leipzig
ISBN: 978-3-8443-2940-7

Imprint (only for USA, GB)

Bibliographic information published by the Deutsche Nationalbibliothek: The Deutsche Nationalbibliothek lists this publication in the Deutsche Nationalbibliografie; detailed bibliographic data are available in the Internet at http://dnb.d-nb.de.

Any brand names and product names mentioned in this book are subject to trademark, brand or patent protection and are trademarks or registered trademarks of their respective holders. The use of brand names, product names, common names, trade names, product descriptions etc. even without a particular marking in this works is in no way to be construed to mean that such names may be regarded as unrestricted in respect of trademark and brand protection legislation and could thus be used by anyone.

Cover image: www.ingimage.com

Publisher: LAP LAMBERT Academic Publishing GmbH & Co. KG
Dudweiler Landstr. 99, 66123 Saarbrücken, Germany
Phone +49 681 3720-310, Fax +49 681 3720-3109
Email: info@lap-publishing.com

Printed in the U.S.A.
Printed in the U.K. by (see last page)
ISBN: 978-3-8443-2940-7

I would like to dedicate this book to the memory of Thomas Anthony Barbera Sr., brother-of-my-heart, July 12, 1948—February 13, 2008; to my sisters Joyce, Margaret, Laura, and Faith; to my brothers Barney and Jack; and to my parents Giacoma and Baldassare, and thank them for their unwavering love and support.

Acknowledgements

I would like to thank Carolyn Kenny, my chair and educator extraordinaire, who, through her guidance, support, and trust in me, provided a model of how beauty, truth, and justice make transformational learning possible. I would like to thank Laura Shapiro, who broke through hard ground with her original arts-based research, making it possible for me to walk in her footsteps for my own inquiry. I would like to thank Laurien Alexandre for her vision of leadership education and the benefits that vision has manifested in my life and learning. I would like to thank Maxine Greene for the inspiration she has given me and so many others in education to apply the power of the imagination toward social justice. I would like to thank Rebecca Hosmer, my copy editor, and Matthew Swerdloff, my technologist, for their constant support and dedication to my work's publication, without which it would not have been possible. Finally, I want to thank my students for their courage and authentic expressions. I have learned so much from them.

TABLE OF CONTENTS

List of Figures

5

8

Chapter I: Introduction

I see the past, present, and future existing all at once before me.

(Blake, as cited in Erdman, 1997, p. 59)

Figure 1.1. My Great Grandmother, Eugina Martinelli.

I Am From

I am from Italian blood.

I am from Sicilian blood.

I am from Gypsy blood.

I am from Grandmothers and Great Grandmothers.

I am from Eugina, Lara, Mandalena, Angelina, and Margarita.

I am from Taconda, Martinelli, Arpino, Ruggerio, and Gulata.

I am from Grandfathers and Great Grandfathers.

I am from Luigi, Nicolasanta, Baldessare, and Colegero.

I am from Cisternino.

I am from Barbera.

I am from Brooklyn,

Where I was called "Black Barbarian Gypsy",

I am from a family of ten.

I am from not enough food.

I am from using a hair dryer to keep warm.

I am from no shelter.

I am from being dispossessed.

I am from a father who worked hard but could not find us a place to live.

I am from no one wanting "*that many kids*" running around their rental apartments.

I am from "You have too many children"!

I am from living in a van.

I am from washing in a wading pool in the city park.

I am from "homelessness" before it was on the evening news.

I am from a mother who had no money for food but fed my artistic spirit with beauty and love.

I am from always being different.

I am from telling my mother "I want to be like everyone else."

I am from her response: "*Oh no*, you don't!"

I am from working on behalf of children who suffer silently.

I am from exposing their subtle and blatant oppressions.

I am from advocating for parents who have not learned how to advocate for themselves.

I am from dedicating my life to helping others.

I am from art for dialogue, transformation, and healing.

I am from art for leading (from the fringes).

I am from art for leading (from my center).

I am from art for leading (for social justice for all).

(Barbera, autoethnographic journal, 2006a, p. 5)

In mid-October 2008, within a week of beginning to write this work, I had a dream: I am standing in a packed auditorium at the podium preparing to deliver my project. As I begin to speak, I look out into the audience and see my mother, Jacqueline (Giacoma), who passed away in 1997. Next to her, to her right is her mother, my grandmother, Angelina Ruggerio. Next to her, on her left, is my mother's grandmother on her father's side, Eugina Martinelli, my Romani/Gypsy great grandmother, who is memorialized in the painting/collage above. I see more faces I recognize from photographs, legends, and tales told to me by my mother, only they are not frozen in sepia photographs, but animated, audible, full of excitement, and in vibrant color. I recognize, too, my grandmother, on my father's side, Mandalena Arpino, and my

10

father's grandmother on his father's side, Margarita Gulata from old photographs of them that I had seen.

By now, I am beginning to recognize a pattern; the entire front row of the auditorium is filled with my grandmothers, great grandmothers and great-great grandmothers. But, the real surprise comes when I realize, as I look out over the entire auditorium as far back as I can see, that hundreds of my grandmothers, generation upon generation, are present as well. All of my maternal ancestors are listening and waiting in anticipation and excitement to hear what I am about to say. I am honored, humbled, and overcome with emotion. Then, I wonder in the eternal time of which dreams are made, "How is it that I am up here with my ancient precious grandmothers as *my* students? Isn't it I who should be *their* student? Isn't what I come to teach, after all, what I have learned from them—from their lives, their stories of pain and sacrifice, their heroic journeys, and their unending love?" In the next moment, I awake in tears of awe and gratitude. I have had an "audience" with my grandmothers, which has given me hope that I may be worthy of their legacy and a conduit of their wisdom to the world.

Greene (1995) says:

A reflective grasp of our life stories and of our ongoing quests, that reaches beyond where we have been, depends on our ability to remember things past. It is against the backdrop of those remembered things and the funded meanings to which they gave rise, that we grasp and understand what is now going on around us. (p. 20)

My ultimate goal as a social justice teacher educator is to demonstrate teaching and learning through authentic engagement in the arts to support education that is libratory, transformational, and considers issues of equity of primary concern. Authentic engagement, for me, requires a prerequisite exploration of my own life history/"her story" to identify the roots of my engagement and commitment to social justice. Because authentic engagement in the exploration of identity is something I will urge my students to do, I believe it is critically important for me to do as well. My engagement in identity exploration serves as a concrete example for my students, in viewing the past in relation to the present, and using the insights gained to help make meaning of what is currently "going on around us."

The social justice classroom is the logical meeting place of the past, present, and future for aspiring teacher educators. By reflecting on the past, students situate

11

themselves more potently in the present, and by awakening to and naming *what is* and *releasing their imagination* to vision *what can be* (Greene, 1995) students are empowered and committed to their vision for change for the future.

Figure 1.2. Lucy Barbera (center) listens as her student tells about her life.

Suominen (2006), a social justice education researcher, feels that for social justice educators, engaging in self-study and exposing our multi-dimensional lives to our students is essential for authentic learning to result. She encourages educators to teach *who they are* (Goodson & Numan, 2002). The following quote from Suominen's autoethnographic journal, titled, "Teaching," encapsulates the essence of her goal to teach equity, critical awareness, acceptance and understanding of diversity *through the arts*:

> You have met them in the space between you and them, because if you don't . . . there is no learning, only memorizing. You have to reveal yourself to your students, because if you don't, they won't believe you. If I want to teach, for me, for the teacher, the option of staying anonymous doesn't exist. (2006, pp. 151-152)

Figure 1.3. Lucy Barbera "Teaching Who She Is."

Kenny (2006) says "as we reveal ourselves to one another, we are found" (p. 159). Kenny, like Dissanayake (1992), sees art as a human birthright and beauty as essential to life:

> The sense of art, that sensibility which is difficult to name, but natural as the light of day or the darkness of night, creates integration, coherence, and strength. . . . This feeling of coherence, integration, and strength arrives through [the] perception of beauty. (2006, p. 158)

Carolyn Kenny's *sense of art* will be the muse guiding this study.

The Study

This study brings together many disparate disciplines. Teacher education is united with social justice education, and both are conjoined with the arts to support leadership and change. How these various disciplines intersect and work to support each other will be the topic of my book. In the following pages, I will discuss each of these disciplines and how they can be (re)united at the service of justice. As an arts-informed ethnographic/autoethnographic study, the method I will employ to do this will be arts-based as well. I will be studying the culture and learning that is generated when social justice teacher education is infused with the arts. Not only do I use the arts as a pedagogical tool to teach social justice, but also as a research tool to understand the unique aspects of this approach to social justice teacher education.

In this study, I will explore the potential for the arts to invigorate social justice teacher education. The purpose for the study is to learn about the culture created when the arts are used to identify, explore, and address social justice issues in the context of a teacher education course. As a teacher educator involved in teaching a social justice course over the last three summers, I am positioned emicly and eticly in this study to investigate the multiple dimensions that will address the gap or, more accurately, to bulk up the scant, though exceptional, literature in the field regarding the utilization of the arts in social justice teacher education.

The Epistemology of Aesthetics

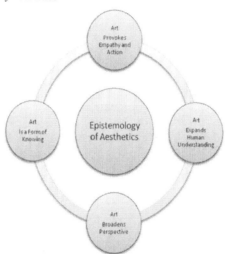

Figure 1.4. The dimensions of the epistemology of aesthetics (adapted from Eisner, 2008).

The epistemology of aesthetics is the leitmotif of this study. In this epistemological paradigm, the arts provide information, understanding, and knowledge, and in this capacity provide a legitimate source of data to the researcher. The epistemology of aesthetics, unlike positivistic epistemologies, allows for the inclusion of diverse realities, pluralistic constructs, and uncertainty. Research method, analysis, and interpretation are seen as an art—rather than a science—that recognizes subjectivity's role and abandons the quest for objectivity.

14

Cole and Knowles (2008), in their *Handbook of the Arts in Qualitative Research*, frame the arts as a rich source of dynamic methods for social science research. Contributors to their text demonstrate how the arts (from collage and video, to sculpture, dance, and installation art) are used as revelatory research methodologies. Eisner (2008) believes that the arts as research tools "contribute to the enlargement of human understanding" (p. 11). He sees art as a vehicle that can enhance our understanding and, when used as a conduit for sense and feeling, (two elements traditionally left out of scientific, particularly quantitative, inquiry) broaden the definition for valid modes of inquiry.

What sets the arts apart as a source of understanding and knowing, according to Eisner (2008), is its ability to express what is "felt," as well as what is directly observed. "Through art," he says, "we come to feel, very often, what we cannot see directly" (p. 8). For Eisner, the arts have multiple contributions to make to the construction of knowledge and of knowing itself. He credits the arts for their ability to reveal nuances, evoke feeling—primarily empathy as a means to understanding—and activate "new ways with which to perceive and interpret the world, ways that make vivid realities that would otherwise go unknown" (p. 11).

Teacher Education, Leadership, and the Arts

I believe that the greatest hope for meaningful and lasting school reform lies with teachers, not necessarily with school administrators. Administrators are struggling to reach a bar dictated by federal mandates that are, in many ways, out of touch with the realities of teaching, learning, and leading in 21st century schools. Many theorists agree that educational reform is most successful when *teachers* are leading it (Bullough & Baughman, 1997; Bullough & Pinnegar, 2001; Childs-Bowen & Moller, 2000; Ciuffetelli-Parker, Fazio, Volante, & Cherubini, 2008; Elstad, 2008; Foster & St. Hilaire, 2004; Lattimer, 2007; McGhan, 2002; Rapp, 2002; Ross, Bradley Cousins, Gadalla, & Hannay, 1999; Rowley, 1988; Urbanski & Nickolaou, 1997). I believe that teachers can and do take initiative for leadership at the grass roots level for social justice in their classrooms and schools every day.

To support these valiant leadership efforts and to add an essential skill base to the field, I believe that wedding teacher education and social justice to the arts is critical. The focus of this book is on teacher education and, in particular, social justice teacher education. I want to explore how the arts can be utilized to facilitate social justice education, in order to catalyze renewed commitment and approaches to leadership for social justice action in schools.

Last year, when I reviewed the literature on social justice teacher education, I observed a disconcerting trend. There was a dearth of literature demonstrating the use of the arts in social justice teacher education. So, although social justice teacher education was alive and well, the arts were not being utilized at the service of social justice teacher education. There were, however, some interesting exceptions that I will briefly describe here.

Because nationally, Art education standards include the use of the arts for cultural understanding and appreciation, it is logical that *art teacher education* programs would include the use of the arts for understanding and appreciation of cultural diversity. Thus, I found that the majority of teacher education programs intentionally using the arts at the service of social justice education fell under the rubric of *Art teacher education.*

This phenomenon is elegantly exemplified in Noel's (2003) creative work in art teacher education. Noel demonstrated socially transformative education using an arts-based approach to multicultural education that engaged her students in "multicultural critical pedagogy which challenge[d] them not only to examine their own beliefs about society, but also to create artistic visions that will inspire others to take up the project of social transformation" (p. 15). Noel's research revealed how her students' made social justice a part of their identities as future teachers and deepened their understanding as it was expressed *through their art.*

Two other very striking exceptions include the research of Shapiro (2004, 2006), with whom I was privileged to work during her groundbreaking dissertation research, and Kenny (1998), my dissertation chair, whose work with First Nation teacher education provides a cogent model for social justice teacher education *through* the arts.

Shapiro (2004, 2006), working with women educational leaders and classroom teachers, revealed the enormous potential of the arts to disrupt the status quo by tapping the emotions to facilitate inquiry and promote leadership for social justice in schools. Shapiro sees the arts as tools that allow for the expression of emotion, capitalizing on the symbolic power of the arts (in contrast to the purely linguistic) to give school leaders deeper insights regarding their social justice work in schools. She posits that:

16

Artmaking can facilitate a personal, authentic engagement with social justice issues and provide opportunities for nonlinguistic meaning-making, which opens up emotions and ideas that cannot easily be accessed in other ways. Artmaking can provide expression of subjective experiences that are important in our lives as leaders. (2006, p. 236)

Kenny (1998), working in First Nations teacher education, presents a framework for native/aboriginal teacher education emphasizing the timeless role the arts play in it. Through the pedagogical approaches used in her teacher development program, Kenny returns to her students the vital gift of their culture to bring to their own teaching; by re-collecting cultural wisdom practices and re-claiming, re-minding, and re-teaching students to use nature and the arts in their teaching practice to re-vivify and teach, using ancient wisdom in modern times, where it is just as much needed than it was in the past.

As a teacher educator myself, I connected not only with the pedagogical practices of performance as ritual, arts and identity, arts as inquiry tool, and arts and community building (to name just a few), that Kenny (1998) sets forth. Also, and seminal to this paper, I was inspired by the practice of the documentation of the process of developing and teaching such practices. This is a model from which others may draw inspiration from the methods used to develop, chronicle, and replicate aesthetic pedagogical practices.

Altogether, with these rare exceptions, the literature I reviewed revealed little related to use of the arts as pedagogical tools for social justice teacher education. I believe this indicates an urgent need to build on the research cited and initiate further development and research to explore and design models using the arts for social justice teacher education.

Social Imagination and Palpable Pedagogy

Greene (2007a) posits that:

Authentic encounters with [the] arts can open windows for teachers and enable them to envision new possibilities for meeting the demands of a moment marked by deep uncertainties and fearful offences against what most of us consider to be decent, humane, and just. (p. 1)

I believe that teachers' social imagination (Greene, 1995) is developed through an authentic engagement with the arts. The expressive arts provide a vehicle for

17

emotions and the accompanying feelings they generate (through visual image making, ritual, song, music, and movement) to catalyze action for change.

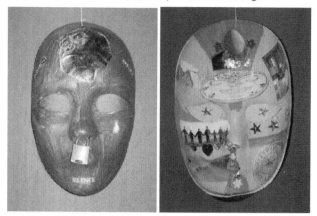

Figure 1.5. Front and back of student mask: Oppression and liberation.

In describing "social imagination," Greene (1995) says:

Social imagination: [is] the capacity to invent visions of what should be and what might be in our deficient society, on the streets where we live, in our schools. . . . We acknowledge the harshness of situations only when we have in mind another state of affairs in which things would be better. (p. 5)

Used as pedagogical tools, I believe the arts can provide vital assistance in developing the capacity to envision a just world by releasing the social imagination (Greene, 1995) for social justice leadership and change that Greene encourages. As a teacher educator and artist researcher, I want to discover how the arts can be utilized to reclaim humanity (Dissanayake, 1992; Eisner, 2008; Kenny, 2006) and to envision and lead change to address social justice issues in schools and the world.

Giroux (2006) sees an urgent need for educators to take responsibility to develop pedagogy that is moral, rather than just technical, to engage students in issues of social justice. He says:

Intellectuals who inhabit our nation's universities should represent the conscience of American society because they not only shape the conditions under which future generations learn about themselves and their relations to others and the outside world, but also because they engage pedagogical practices that are, by their very nature, moral and political rather than simply technical. Pedagogy in this instance works to shift how students think about the

18

issues affecting their lives and the world at large, potentially energizing them to seize such moments as possibilities for acting on the world and for engaging it as a matter of politics, power, and social justice. (p. 66)

As a social justice teacher educator, I am well positioned to answer the call to develop engaging pedagogical practices that nurture not only social imagination (Greene, 1995), but oppositional imaginations (Rapp, 2002) as well, to address the moral and political issues affecting my students, my students' students, their classrooms, their schools, and the world. Rapp says that students' "repeated and varied exposure to the arts" (p. 237) is critical to developing their commitment to social justice. "Artists," Rapp says, "offer explanations that can serve as windows into the haunting nature of unfulfilled promises and destinies that affect each one of us" (p. 237). Significantly, the expressive arts, when used as pedagogical tools provide *both* verbal *and* nonverbal methods to do this by identifying and exposing, exploring and inquiring about, and addressing and redressing social justice issues that my students (as current and future teachers) will encounter in their schools.

Charmaz (2005) succinctly outlines the dimensional and inclusive scope of what attention to social justice involves:

> An interest in social justice means attentiveness to ideas and actions concerning fairness, equity, equality, democratic processes, status, hierarchy, and individual and collective rights and obligations. . . . It means exploring tensions between complicity and consciousness, choice and constraint, indifference and compassion, inclusion and exclusion, poverty and privilege, and barriers and opportunities. (p. 507)

Shapiro's (2004) commitment to the arts for fostering attentiveness concerning fairness includes identifying sites of social injustice in schools, from the cafeteria to the boardroom, and locating sites of blatant and subtle oppression in schools. Shapiro's expanded vision includes arts as a community engagement tool with school leaders creating:

> Spaces for all members of their school communities, including teachers, parents, and students, to tell their own stories [where] artmaking activities . . . can be incorporated into faculty meetings, study groups, and professional development programs. (p. 247)

The expressive arts provide social justice educators what I call *palpable pedagogy* that focuses attention of this caliber on critical justice issues and galvanizes action for equity for which Charmaz (2005), Giroux (2006), Shapiro (2004), and Rapp (2002) advocate.

PALPABLE PEDAGOGY

Figure 1.6. Model of palpable pedagogy.

In this study, I propose that the arts provide *palpable pedagogy* for social justice teacher educators. That is, pedagogy that allows learning to be visible, visceral, tactile, kinesthetic, and sensory; to be experienced, felt, and observed phenomenologically. *Palpable pedagogy* integrates art processes and learning, allowing emotion to be generated, felt, and channeled to motivate learners to action. *Palpable pedagogy* is critical pedagogy, in that it is used to uncover and disrupt power imbalances. *Palpable pedagogy* is reciprocal, communal, touchable, graspable, and tangible. *Palpable pedagogy* manifests itself in a painting, college, mural, poetry, drama, narrative, dance/movement, or music/song; it is experienced alone or in tandem as a *creative connection* (Rogers, 1993). *Palpable pedagogy* utilizes the expressive arts to provide educators, in their role as social change leaders, along with their students, with powerful tools for inquiry, identification, examination, and redress for social justice issues to rectify oppressive practices and experiences of students and teachers in schools.

The following excerpt from my teaching journal shows one example of how the arts provide *palpable pedagogy* in social justice teacher education.

Figure 1.7. Polarities: Inclusion—Exclusion.

Parade of images: The students have just presented their "Parade of Images" (Boal, 1979), a psycho-dramatic tableau, illustrating the student-generated polarities. Each student gets a chance to body sculpt the others in their group, (allowing for an "embodiment" of the polarities) then the next, then the next, till a parade of images is generated representing, for instance, oppression then liberation or inclusion-exclusion. Again, as the students process what they have just experienced, "conversation fragments" catch my breath, a rich sound collage of students simultaneously expressing revelations that the creative process unleashed reflected in an auditory gestalt of their learning.

Amazing how much information I got without saying a word . . .

Opened up the nonverbal because there was no dialogue . . . (Barbera, teaching journal, 2006c, p. 7)

Identity, Dialogue, and Reflection in Social Justice Education

Numerous researchers (Brown, 2006; Clark, 2005; Day, C., 2002; Goodson & Numan, 2002; Hatton, 1998; Kenny, 1998; LaBoskey, 2006; Lynn & Smith, 2007; Noel, 2003; Rodgers, 2006; Suominen, 2006) currently working and researching in the field of social justice education, have identified several key components necessary for effective social justice teacher education. According to these researchers, effective social justice education must include the exploration of self/identity, structured dialogue, and reflection. In my work as a social justice teacher educator—at first, unconsciously, later, more consciously and inspired by social justice educators (Greene, 1995; Katz & Ryan, 2005; Kenny, 1998; Shapiro, 2004, 2006), I designed these

21

components into my teaching to maximize student understanding and application of social justice pedagogy.

In addition, I have added the use of the expressive arts to my work in social justice teacher education, to energize these effective components and bring them to life in my students' lives and practices. In the following section, I will present examples from my research of these key elements (identity, reflection, and dialogue) for effective social justice education (as cited above), and their transformation to *palpable pedagogy* when fused with the arts.

Identity

It's 3:15 p.m. and my teaching plan says I should be introducing Parker Palmer's (1998) *Movement Model for Social Change* and have students place themselves on a continuum regarding their commitment to social change action. My intention was for students to engage in a pre-course self-assessment using his model and at the end of the course do a post-assessment to capture progress along the social change continuum.

Figure 1.8. Educational autobiography.

However, the students are still involved in processing/sharing the multi-modal "educational autobiographies" assigned for homework during the introductory class. The student energy for this is moving decidedly forward and I think it would not be useful to disrupt the flow. One student is singing "*Somewhere Over the Rainbow*" in an acapella of exquisite tones as an extension of her autobiographical collage. Everyone in the room turns away from what they are doing to look and listen. (Barbera, teaching journal, 2006c, pp. 5-6)

Figure 1.9. Student sharing her educational autobiography.

Figure 1.10. Extension of educational autobiography: Student singing "Somewhere Over the Rainbow."

Figure 1.11. Students explore and dialogue about ability and disability.

Student Action Plan Presentation: Taking the "Diss" Out of Disability

This is an exemplary plan. The students who designed this plan included five different modalities (body tracing, collage, *parade of images*, lifted poem, and word web) that work very well together to bring the participant into relationship with their own lives and the lives of people with disability by looking at "ability" as a continuum, rather than a static way of being. Students are partnered up and they are tracing each other's silhouettes on large sheets of roll paper. They are asked to illustrate their body tracing by thinking of a time in their lives when they themselves may have felt "disabled" in some way. Dialogue fragments generated from this exercise follow:

This was my journey with my husband, what he felt, I felt.

Diagnosis—best guess.

Giving support—choices.

I was told I'd never have children. It was very painful.

I was discriminated against.

Anxiety affects me professionally and personally. Fear is a very bad thing—I felt very frightened of people.

I remember that disabled feeling, that feeling of exile.

The way I was brought up was to ultimate failure.

I'm gonna offer my hand regardless.

In order to get here, we had to go there.

It helps me in my field to develop my empathy skills, I've been there.

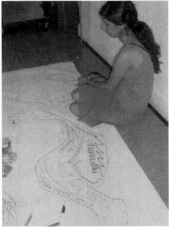

Figure 1.12. Body trace and self-exploration on disability.

We take for granted things we do everyday.

The body tracing had to do with medical issues.

What did you learn about your own perceptions about disabilities?

When my husband became disabled, he was no longer considered a professional. He no longer knew who he was. He was lost, angry. He was grieving his loss. We were both able to do it together.

What is this teaching us about ability?

Figure 1.13. Lucy Barbera (left) joins student dialogue group, 2007.

One of the presentation team members wraps up the activity with this statement:

> We have to reconstruct the norm of what we see people as. Disability and power are connected. If you are normal, you have power. If you are not normal, you don't. We (the Action Plan Group) want that to be seen and to be changed. (Barbera, teaching journal, 2006c, pp. 18-20)

Figure 1.14. Student uses movement to demonstrate personal ability.

Touchstones: The students have been working on their *Touchstones* (DeCantias, 1996), a sculpture made from natural objects, something to remind them of the social justice

work they are committed to doing in the world when they go back to their lives outside the protected walls of this classroom. I encourage students to journal about their Touchstone when they are finished assembling it. I suggest they reflect upon and dialogue with their piece and give it a voice. (Barbera, teaching journal, 2006c, pp. 29-33)

Following are some of these reflections:

I will take back the joy of artwork and the power of creativity. The reverence for myself and my companions. The understanding of myself better. The beauty and joy of collaboration and the collective. My relationship with myself. . . . The power of metaphor. Understanding others. A holistic integration of compartmentalized pieces of my being. Confidence in myself. Understanding of myself. (F.G., student journal entry, 2006)

Figure 1.15. Student's Touchstone.

I reiterate to the students that the Touchstones can act as reminders (DeCantias, 1996) of what they desire to take back to the world with them from this class. I ask the students to allow their Touchstones to inspire them and to journal their inspirations. (Barbera, teaching journal, 2006c, pp. 29-33)

Some additional responses from student journals follow:

What I will take back with me from this class to the world is belief and affirmation that I have the skills to open eyes and hearts for change. I am from doubt and questioning. I am from being touched by the opportunity to express myself through art and poetry. I am from bringing the power of expression and opening of the heart. I am form opening the heart to embracing possibility. (W.J., student journal entry, 2006)

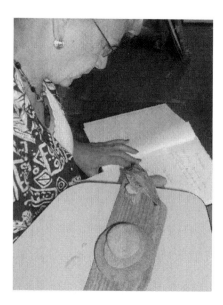

Figure 1.16. Student reflects on her Touchstone.

Every time I look at my Touchstone, I will be reminded of where I want to be. I will get the messages I am sending myself. I need to work on taking that lid off my emotions and release my creativity when solving problems or facing issues. (E.F., student journal entry, 2006)

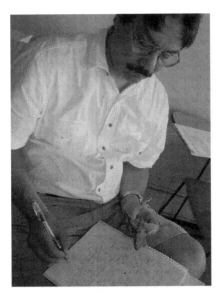

Figure 1.17. Journal reflection on Touchstone.

What I will take back to the world with me is a greater awareness of how powerful art is in expressing thoughts, ideas, emotions and how I will use this knowledge to share my feelings and get others to share theirs with me. (K.K., student journal entry, 2006)

What I'll take back with me to the world: A sense of wonder, a sense of empowerment. My task: to share it. (C.G.M., student journal entry, 2006)

What I'll take back with me to the world is the ability to foster social change and leadership. (P.B., student journal entry, 2006)

What I'll take back with me to the world is the knowledge that through my own ability and freedom to create, I can help others empower themselves towards emotional liberation and potential to initiate change. (A.B., student journal entry, 2006)

I will take back with me a better world that we helped make together

I will take the eyes, ears, tears, and fears of everyone I encounter to help empower them. The conviction that change for social justice is attainable is what I will take away with me. I know I am equipped to do my part and recognize opportunity. (D.C., student journal entry, 2006)

The Crisis of Representation—Art as a Form of Knowledge

At this juncture, the reader may feel they have wandered into a new territory, a place where a poem, painting, sculptural form, dialogue fragment, or dramatic act are now supplying them with information that, in the past, they derived solely through a written narrative or quantitatively, through number, chart, and graph. Typically, research has been presented using the scientific model and there is an almost unconscious acclimation to this mode of representation that associates it with unequivocal truth. However, as already stated, understanding and knowledge are formed in many ways.

The arts provide ways of knowing and understanding not obtainable by other means and are capable of representing truths inaccessible by any other form. Gadamer, Weinsheimer, and Marshall (2004) say that art opens us to "modes of experience in which a truth is communicated that cannot be verified by methodological means proper to science," (p. xxi) and "through a work of art a truth is experienced that we cannot attain in any other way" (pp. xxi-xxii). As the epistemology of aesthetics is more fully developed in subsequent chapters, the connection between aesthetic ideas and beauty's connection to morality and justice will be explored more fully.

Art as Process

In this ethnographic study, not only do the arts function to assist us in developing a fuller interpretation and understanding of the culture of the other (my students and myself), they also provide personal meaning making, synthesizing, and pedagogical tools. However, as pedagogical tools, the expressive arts (such as music, movement, poetry, painting, mask-making, drama, collage, and sculpture) are used not so much to create a fine art *product* to be hung in a gallery, although it very well may be one day. For the purposes of this study, the expressive arts are used as tools with which to understand, inquire about, locate and explore feelings, ask essential questions, identify paradoxes, create visions, and imagine alternatives. Keeping the focus on the *process* of exploration *through the art process*, the use of the arts for expression and discovery is primary. In this way, undertaking the expressive arts process is possible for

30

artists and non-artists alike. Unlike the fine arts, where the focus is on the formal elements of the work produced and, consequently, often on the *product* itself, the focus with the expressive arts is on the *process*, with the intention to explore ideas, emotions, essential questions, and possible solutions *through the process of art-making,* and not necessarily the *production* of a work of art.

Summary

To recapitulate, the purpose of this book is to explore how the arts and especially the expressive arts, and the creative intelligence they tap and foster, can be used to facilitate leadership development for social justice in the context of teacher education, in order to catalyze, renew, and solidify commitment for social justice action in schools. Greene (1995) sees the arts as facilitating breakthroughs, as imagination builders, and as opening new ways of being and seeing that allow for the unexpected. These are the very skills that leadership theorists Bennis (1994), Gardner (1995), Heifetz (1994), Vaill (1989), and others posit as indispensible to effective leadership. This paper is designed to illustrate the power engendered when the arts are employed in teacher training for social justice to create *palpable pedagogy* and a new model for social justice teacher education.

The dimensions of *palpable pedagogy,* along with the key elements for effective social justice education, and teacher education for leadership and change, will be explored, revealed, (re)joined, and supported in this study. Additionally, an exploration of the arts as a legitimate form of representation and knowledge will be expanded and the study will be framed in its entirety by the epistemology of aesthetics and a *new* model for social justice teacher education, inclusive of the arts, will be proposed.

In this chapter, I have outlined the purpose, questions, and rationale for this study in the context of the epistemology of aesthetics and included some examples of the particular language of art and the kind of teaching, learning and knowing that art engenders. In chapter 2, I will explore this phenomenon further and frame my study through the review of literature in the context of previous research and the expansive epistemology of aesthetics, arguing the validity of my research topic and questions. In chapter 3, I will expand on my topic and describe my research methodology giving a rationale for selecting the aesthetic methods I employ, along with supporting literature, and demonstrate my familiarity and dexterity using aesthetic means for the context and content of my study to demonstrate sufficient mastery of the arts-based ethnographic methods I employ for my research for this study. In chapter 4, I will present the findings and results of my research. In chapter 5, I will present my autoethnography/study of the culture of self as college professor using the arts to teach social justice. In chapter 6, I will discuss my conclusions, and in chapter 7, I will discuss the implications of my research for leadership and change.

Chapter II: Literature Review

In this chapter, I will elaborate on the epistemology of aesthetics through the review of literature in this field, examine works seminal to the study of social justice education through the arts for leadership and change, and present the previous research in the context of my argument for a *palpable pedagogy* for social justice teacher education; where arts are used to vitalize, humanize, and inspire pre-service and current teachers to teach and lead for change. My literature review will be presented in five interrelated sections as follows.

The roots of art, beauty, justice, and humanity: In this section, in non-chronological fashion, I will explicate the philosophical roots of the wedding of beauty and justice via Scarry (1999), beauty and the ethical of Plato and art's connection to the moral, experienced in medieval times and in the philosophy of John Dewey (1934). I will examine anthropological themes supporting the bio/behavioral beginnings of the arts as a human necessity elucidated by ethnologist, Ellen Dissanayake (1990, 1992, 2000).

1. Aesthetic education: In this section, I will explore aesthetic education, particularly of Greene (1995, 2007a-h) and Eisner (1991, 2002a-b, 2008).

2. Critical theory and humanistic education: In this section, I will discuss the philosophy and pedagogy of critical theory in education, via Giroux (2001, 2006), Giroux and Giroux (2004), and Bell and Schneidewind's (1987) vision for an integration of humanistic education and critical theory.

3. Multicultural Art teacher education: In this section, I will more thoroughly examine the recent work in multicultural art teacher education of Jana Noel (2003).

4. Arts-based teacher education and the arts and social justice in adult education: In this section, I will review models of arts-based social justice teacher education in the work of Kenny (2006) and Shapiro (2004, 2006), and discuss new developments in arts-based social justice adult and community education compiled by Clover and Stalker (2007).

5. Aesthetic leadership: In closing, Ladkin (2008) and Hansen, Ropo, and Sauer (2007) offer a contemporary vision of beauty and leadership that begs to be explored in this literature review, as the river of thought presented thus far naturally flows toward it, in the context of the topic of my paper, "Expressive Art, Leadership, and Change in Social Justice Education."

33

Therefore, I have chosen to end my literature review with an examination of this intriguing juxtaposition.

The Roots of Art, Beauty, Justice, and Humanity

"Folded into the uneven aesthetic surfaces of the world is a pressure toward social equality" (Scarry, 1999, p. 110). I believe the joining of the beautiful and the creative imagination with the ethical, and the joining of the ethical to purpose and action for justice is germane to the argument for the use of arts for social justice education. Therefore, I will examine these connections here. Equations between beauty and truth in poetry and philosophy abound—across cultures from Plato's philosophical tenants, to American Indian cosmology, through the Middle Ages. Keats (1819), in his Ode on a Grecian Urn, rhapsodized "Beauty is truth, truth beauty, that is all Ye know on earth, and all ye need to know."

Dewey (1934) says that "art is more moral than moralities" (p. 362) and places the locus of moral and ethical conscience with poets. "The moral prophets of humanity have always been poets even though they spoke in free verse or by parable" (p. 362). Dewey, in his philosophical treatise, *Art as Experience*, urges a recovery and integration of aesthetic experience with "normal processes of living" (p. 9). In joining the aesthetic to humanness, Dewey theorizes that

> Esthetic experience is always more than esthetic. In it a body of matters and meanings, not in themselves esthetic, *become* esthetic as they enter into an ordered rhythmic movement toward consummation. The material itself is widely human. . . . The material of esthetic experience in being human—human in connection with the nature of which it is a part—is social. (p. 339)

For Dewey (1934), aesthetic experience is a form of human life, a history, a record of life, and "a means of promoting its development" (p. 339). Like Dewey, Eco (2000) refers to beauty as human experience. Eco contends that Medievals did not abstract beauty, but related to beauty in "everyday feelings, to lived experience" (p. 4) and a "moral reality" (p. 5).

Ladkin (2008), writing about leading beautifully, harkens back to the Platonic sense of beauty as an essence that magnetizes beauty to what is good and true. Ladkin says, "The link Plato makes between beauty and purified mind and which Plotinus makes between beauty and the soul necessitates the connection between beauty and the good. By Plato's definition, beauty cannot be used for bad ends" (p. 34).

34

Navajo professor of anthropology, Witherspoon (1977), in his analysis of the Navajo term for beauty, *hozho*, says that "This term means much more than 'beauty' or 'beautiful conditions'. . . . [it's] everything that the Navajo thinks of as being good—that is, good as opposed to evil, favorable to man as opposed to unfavorable" (p. 23).

Indeed, Witherspoon (1977), reflecting on a universal principle of American Indian culture, says that "the goal of Navajo life in this world is to live to maturity in the condition described as hozho" (p. 25). It is beauty, too, says Scarry (1999) in her essay, "On Beauty and Being Just," which " . . . intensifies the pressure we feel to repair existing injuries" (p. 57). For Scarry, beauty compels us to seek the truth and is the "starting place for education" (p. 31).

Scarry (1999) argues against beauty's banishment from the humanities under several false political arguments. One argument against beauty she cites is that beauty dulls our awareness, pacifies us, and, by doing so, turns us away from social injustice. Far from being true, Scarry says, beauty develops our power of observation and our ability to notice details, which sharpen our ability to identify injustice when we encounter it. Scarry explains it thus

> There is no way to be in a high state of alert toward injustices—to subjects that, because they entail injuries, will bring distress—without simultaneously demanding of oneself precisely the level of perceptual acuity that will forever be opening one to the arrival of beautiful sights and sounds. How will one even notice, let alone become concerned about, the inclusion in a political assembly of only one economic point of view unless one has also attended, *with full acuity*, [italics added] to a debate that is itself a beautiful object, full of arguments, counterarguments, wit, spirit, ripostes, ironies, testing, contesting; and how in turn will one hear the nuances of even this debate unless one also makes oneself available to the songs of birds or poets? (pp. 60-61)

Like Greene (1995), Scarry feels beauty serves us by honing our ability to perceive *what is going on around us* which leads us in turn from the particular (self) to the collective (others) and consequently to what Scarry calls the distributional. In Scarry's (1999) paradigm, beauty urges us to *protect, replicate,* and *share* what is beautiful—including fairness, liberty, and justice. "Equality," she says "is the heart of beauty" (p. 98).

According to Scarry (1999), not only is our power of observation enhanced by beauty, but our will to create beauty is also developed. It is both of these that we bring to bear at the service of justice and propel us to action: "Because beauty repeatedly brings us face-to-face with our own powers to create, we know where and how to locate those powers when a situation for injustice calls on us . . ." (p. 115).

Finally, Scarry (1999) ends her argument where she began. At the outset she characterizes beauty as inspiring replication and in her summary posits that beauty begs to be shared. "Beautiful things," she says, "give rise to the notion of distribution, to a lifesaving reciprocity, to fairness" (p. 95). It is this "lifesaving reciprocity, to fairness" function of the arts to which I strive to expose my students, and why I argue for the use of the arts in social justice teacher education.

In *Homo Aestheticus: Where Art Comes From and Why*, Dissanayake (1992) positions art or what she calls *making special* as a biological behavior essential to human survival. Dissanayake ties the ability to create, or make special, to our humanness, and indeed, to our very humanity. Dissanayake argues that art is a human need, "satisfying of a human need or species trait" (p. 33) with survival value as a behavior because the following biological indicators are present: throughout time humans have been "positively inclined to do it, [because they] spend a great deal of time and effort doing it, [and because of its] universality" (p. 33).

Characterized in this way, art then can be viewed as a birthright and quadrangulated with food, clothing, and shelter as essential to human life. Accepting, as I do, Dissanayake's bio-behavioral interpretation of the origins and evolutionary function of the arts, the question then is "why?" What purpose(s) did the arts serve and are these purposes still relevant today? Dissanayake illuminates this inquiry and indicates that, at their origin, the arts helped with things requiring action. Indeed, she says that the arts were not solely created for their own sake, but served as "enabling mechanisms" (1992, p. 156). How exactly did the arts enable? One of the ways, according to Dissanayake, that the arts enabled humans was to assist them in leaving their ordinary state of consciousness and experience an altered state of reality. Greene (2007b) describes this phenomenon as the power of imagination, that is, the "capacity to break with the ordinary, the given, the taken-for-granted, and open doors to possibility" (p. 1). The fact that the arts could transport us, allowing us respite from daily reality, allowing us to imagine new ways of being and living in the world, did not diminish their value, but added to it. The pleasure and refreshment the arts afforded would then fund ordinary reality by enhancing the ability to *open doors to possibilities,* cope with challenges, solve problems, and join in collective initiatives, and give pleasure, as in Kenny's (1998) *aesthetic arrest*.

Dissanayake (1992) points to the direct correlation between ritual (enACTment) and action, and sees ritual as a sort of prototype of action. She believes that, through ritual, we learn about "doing something" (p. 69) or acting upon something. In addition, Dissanayake juxtaposes the arts and emotion and, like Shapiro (2004, 2006), sees emotion as a catalyst for action. By generating emotion, the arts have a transformational capacity that allows participants structured processes through which they can make meaning, envision change, and take action—even, and especially, in times of uncertainty.

Dissanayake (1992), mocking modern culture, says that "beauty, which used to be indelibly associated with the moral and the social, is now individual and . . . solely in the eye of the beholder and only skin deep" (p. 136). However, I believe that the arts continue to be utilized to build community, foster cooperation and collaboration, and in ritual (as art or making special), to unify and bond individuals and groups, to build common strength for action, and heighten the likelihood of individual and collective success/survival. It is *this* spirit, purpose, and the empowering ancient root of the arts that I strive to harness for social justice teacher education—one that is at "the service of abiding human concerns—ones that engage our feelings in the most profound ways" (Dissanayake, 1992, p. 61) and motivate action for change in the world.

Aesthetic Education

Much has been written about Greene's contributions to and impact on philosophy, the arts, libratory education, educational research, educational reform, and social justice. (Ayers & Miller,1998). Greene (1995) elegantly invites us to re-conceptualize education, by including the imperative for social responsibility assisted by the imagination, through the arts. For this reason, I think it is most appropriate to begin any discussion of aesthetic education as critical pedagogy with Greene. For Greene, "transformative pedagogies must relate both to existing conditions and to something we are trying to bring into being, something that goes beyond a present situation" (p. 51).

Imagination, for Greene (2007e), is "a passion for possibility" (p. 2). It is simultaneously the mediating bridge, vehicle, and fuel that can be tapped to assist in identifying *what is going on* (as critical theory urges us to do), seduce us to imagine an

37

alternative reality—*from what is to what can be*, and propel us to take responsibility to act. Listen to how Greene (2007a) frames it:

> I want mostly to argue for the centrality of imagination because of its power to enable persons to reach towards alternatives, to reach beyond; and I want to argue for the arts because of the ways in which they open windows in experience, provide moments of freedom and presence, enable us to break with terrible moments (that) apathy and numbness keep us, in our ongoing conversations with the young, ardently in the changing a problematic world. (p. 2)

In addition to assisting us in envisioning alternatives, Greene (2007f) says "authentic encounters with the arts" (p. 1) can provide a counterbalance to the indifference and apathy prevalent in schools among teachers and students alike. Drummed down in the unpredictable storm of federal and state mandates obsessed with the technical aspects of education, anxious students and stranded teachers cower under the cudgel of the high stakes of learning standards (standardizations) and testing. Green's clear logic gives hope and direction to educators and teacher educators. Her calm, but passionate reason assures us that there are relevant goals, with human value, that eclipse what can be legislated or measured and the role of the arts in education has not abandoned these goals.

For Greene (2007d), the unity of theory and action (praxis) constitute what she calls "social imagination," and prompts the question, "What can I do to repair, to make it better?" (p. 8) As a teacher educator, I am interested in how Greene's paradigm frames action as *with* the other as she asks

> What can I do *with* [italics added] others? What can I do to share their feeling of their social vision? What can I do to share in the creation of a social vision? . . . What can I do in my classroom? What do I do in my artwork to involve people, shaping a vision of how life might be, and coming together to try to shape some aspect of the world, not the whole world, but the aspects that are close to you, into something closer to the that vision. (p. 9)

The questions Greene (2007e) poses, the vision she engenders, and the pedagogies of thought and imagination she articulates through the making and perceiving of works of art give me hope and inspire me as I create a critical *palpable pedagogy* powered by the arts, to equip my students with tools to support their imagination, inspiration, and provocation to social responsibility and action.

Whether it be in educational theory, curriculum and instruction, educational evaluation, or arts-based research, Eisner (2002a, 2002b), in the fine Deweyan tradition of which Greene is a part, brings aesthetic education into sharp focus as critically important to the development of mind and the person. In Eisner's schema, not only are the arts critical to the development of mind, but they provide a model for education in general as well. Eisner (2002b) argues that "the forms of thinking the arts stimulate and develop are far more appropriate for the real world we live in than the tidy right angled boxes we employ in our schools in the name of school improvement" (p. 11).

Upon examination, the forms of thinking to which Eisner (2002b) refers have a common feature. They are premised on the belief in multiple ways of knowing. I want to discuss briefly the distinctive forms of thinking generated by the arts that Eisner has identified, not only because they provide an argument for the use of the arts in primary and secondary education, but, for the purpose of my paper, because these forms of thinking have obvious value in teacher education *as well as* in the arts-based educational research that I am undertaking.

According to Eisner (2002b), one of the forms of thinking the arts stimulate is an appreciation of qualitative relationships and the quality of judgment making that is the result. "In the arts," Eisner says, "judgments are made in the absence of rule" (p. 5). The value here is that the arts teach how to behave in times of uncertainty, how to appraise options, and change direction if necessary before acting. Eisner frames the development of these capacities as becoming qualitatively intelligent.

The second lesson that can be learned from the arts, Eisner (2002b) posits, is "flexible purposing" (p. 7). This form of thinking allows rigid control and adherence to a plan to be slackened at the service of discovery. The third form of thinking postulates that form and content are bound, which he believes, prompts an extraordinary attention to detail. Eisner says that attention to the particular is important for educators, because "the distinctive character of how we teach is a pervasive aspect of what we teach" (p. 8). Applied to research, this logic supposes that "the form we use to display data shapes its meaning" (p. 8).

For Eisner (2002b), "meaning is not limited to what is assertable" (p. 8), but there are multiple ways to know and they are most definitely not limited to words. As a special form of experience, Eisner says the relationship between our thinking and the material with which we work fosters discovery, more questions, and multiple solutions. The cognitive demands made by different media help us "learn to think within it" and

39

expands our ability to think and act in new ways. Finally, Eisner says, the challenges and ideas an art process or work of art generates give us "a special form of experience" (p. 10) and the "aesthetic satisfaction" (p. 10) that ensues becomes its own reward. In this form, the importance of aesthetic satisfaction becomes the motive for the learning, just as it was in ancient times.

Eisner (2002a) believes the arts have the potential to create a new culture of schooling, vastly different from our current one, which is modeled as it is on industrial culture fixated on mandates, measures, and the management of learning, independent of context. Like Greene, Eisner points out that the arts give permission to engage the imagination as a means for exploring new possibilities and that the critical cognitive function they perform is "to help us learn to *notice* [italics added] the world" (p. 10). To this end, Eisner sagely proposes that the techno/cognitive paradigm of learning currently in mode be replaced with "artistically rooted forms of intelligence" (p. 5), and that education consider for its aim to be "the preparation of artists" (p. 11).

Critical Theory and Humanistic Education

The Frankfurt School, says Giroux (2001), placed critical thinking at the heart of the struggle for freedom and social change. Critical theory brought to public consciousness the inner workings of how institutions reinforce and perpetuate societal power structures and the inequities they breed, as well as an analysis of the distinction between the status quo and the ideal and, equally important, an inquiry into the connection (or disconnection) between change theory and action. Giroux and Giroux (2004) stress the need to include a critical theory focus in education and advocates for pedagogy to "connect learning to social change, scholarship to commitment, and classroom knowledge to public life" (p. 117). Giroux (2001) locates schools as sites of the reinforcement and perpetuation of detrimental inequities in society and, as such, offer a logical "site for creating a critical discourse around forms a democratic society might take and the socio-economic forces that might prevent such forms from emerging" (p. 116).

Giroux (2001) calls for the development of a radical critical pedagogy, a *pedagogy for the opposition*—one that exposes and questions the dominant societal ideology and provides students with the opportunity to grapple with the contradictions in which they are enmeshed as participants in the very system that they are being relied upon to help change. Giroux frames this paradox and the pedagogical potential it contains:

40

Schools produce social formations around class, gender, and racial exploitation, but, at the same time, they contain contradictory pluralities that generate possibilities for mediation and contestation of dominant ideologies and practices. In effect, the school is neither an all-encompassing foothold of domination nor a locus of revolution; thus, it contains ideological and the material spaces for the development of radical pedagogies. (p. 115)

It is just such a space and the development of a radical pedagogy that I hope to plan and implement through the development of *palpable pedagogy* for social justice education.

Bell and Schneidewind (1987) supply a cogent model for such pedagogies by calling for the joining of critical theory with humanistic education. Humanistic education, they contend, with its focus on the personal concern and development of the individual, would be much better served if it joined forces with critical theory to form a truly libratory education focused on the rights and justice of the collective. What humanistic education does so well is to engage students in experientially based learning, allow them self-direction, cooperatively structure learning, and places a focus on the affective dimension of the individual to enhance self-esteem and self-empowerment. What critical theory has to offer education is a thorough analysis of the social and political hierarchical power structures and agendas (capitalism among them) embedded in the very educational institutions in which we strive to educate and liberate students for democratic citizenship and work in the world.

Proposing an integration of the two fields, Bell and Schneidewind (1987) say there is a "need for an expanded societal perspective if the goals of humanistic education are to be met" (p. 58). Critical theory is interested in identifying how the dominant/subordinate relationships that permeate the society as a whole find their way into and replicate themselves in schools as reflected in the school's mission, goals, curriculum, power structure, and even its student assessment practices and how these practices serve to maintain the societal status quo. The pitfall of humanistic educators, Bell and Schneidewind contend, is that they have

Avoided a careful examination of the socializing function of schools and have failed to conduct a thorough analysis of institutional power. Most attribute primary importance to psychological factors that shape people's lives and give little attention to social, economical, political, and historical influences. While self-concept and interpersonal skills are indeed important factors in shaping a

41

person's life, an individual's race, sex, economic status, power, and resources all very much affect a person's well being. (pp. 57-58)

Most educators and social change agents would agree that educational change and societal change are inseparable. However, the two fields positioned to collaborate in this change have remained largely separate. Bell and Schneidewind (1987) say that critical theorists fault both the "student-centered curriculum and multicultural education for focusing on consensus and harmony, rather than dealing with the conflict and dominant and subordinate power relations" (p. 61). Critical theorists posit that the hidden curriculum and the daily school day realities of power-over support the status quo, benefitting the economic and social agenda of the dominant society. Bell and Schneidewind grasp the challenge and solution, reminiscent of Freire (1972), through praxis and continued dialogue between the two camps:

> Both humanistic education and critical theory fail to grapple sufficiently with the dialectical process of theory and practice, the personal and social, cognition and affect. In the attempt to deal with these contradictions on its own, each approach falls short. Current work in these two areas, however, leans toward a synthesis that could be furthered through dialogue. (p. 73)

Bell and Schneidewind's (1987) integrative model for liberatory education makes a contribution to the call for synthesis by combining personal power and group skills advanced by the humanists with critical awareness and the development of critical consciousness advanced by critical theorists for personal *and* social action for change, thus combining practice and theory. The authors give vibrant examples of the application of their model in the classroom and also cite the work of Shor (1980) and Coover, Deacon, Esser, and Moore (1977) as inspirational to their model. Most of the works Bell (2003a, 2003b) and Schneidewind and Davidson (2006) have authored or coauthored (Adams, Bell, & Griffin, 2007; Roberts, Bell, & Murphy, 2008) since are practice-based handbooks that exemplify the synthesis they envision, providing models for the integration of humanistic education and critical theory for liberatory education. Schneidewind and Davidson (2006) continues to chair the Humanistic Multicultural Education graduate program at SUNY New Paltz, and encouraged me to develop the course that is the topic of this study, "Expressive Arts, Leadership, and Change" for the program. Bell's (in press) most recent work called *Storytelling for Social Justice: Connecting Narrative and the Arts in Antiracist Teaching* is in press. Working with a team of artists and public school teachers, Bell brings her undergraduate students into public schools and demonstrates how the arts can be used to teach about race and racism. Her book details the results of this arts-based project.

As a humanistic teacher educator, I was extremely fortunate to have been mentored by Lee Bell (now teaching at Barnard) and Nancy Schneidewind (still at SUNY, New Paltz), as a graduate student and, now, as an adjunct professor in the Humanistic Multicultural Education Program that they launched over 30 years ago at SUNY, New Paltz. The *palpable pedagogy* that I have researched, proposed, and developed in this paper has its roots in the learning gained while working with them, as well as in the example they have so passionately given me.

Multicultural Art Teacher Education

In addition to arts integration across disciplines (discipline-based arts education), the field of art teacher education has recently produced a rich variety and abundance of research (Darts, 2004; Day, L., 2002; Johnson, 2002; Knipe, 2004) that focuses on the use of the arts for multicultural education awareness and education, cross-cultural studies, and social justice education. Indeed, art teacher education appears to be leading and outpacing all other disciplines in the use of the arts for social justice education in general. Noel's (2003) teaching and research in multicultural art teacher education beautifully exemplifies how the arts can be used to assist students in making meaning of their own identities in relation to the complex the task of "becoming social transformers of society" (p. 15).

Noel's (2003) arts-based approach to art teacher education, seen demonstrated in a graduate course she wrote and taught, is revealed in her article, "Creative Artwork in Response to Issues of Social Justice: A Critical Multicultural Pedagogy." The article excited me because, as I do, Noel believes that the arts provide a powerful pedagogy *and* that the exploration of identity is a critical first step in teaching for social justice. Eisner (2002a) says that "as humans, we are meaning making creatures" and that "meaning is not limited to what words can express" (p. 230). Noel invites her students to explore their identity in the context of prejudice, racism, White silence, and poverty. By allowing students to reflect (through their artwork) on the presence and impact of these themes in their own lives, Noel is hoping her students will develop a deeper awareness of how their own prejudices influenced their identities, which in turn, she believes, can begin to disturb their identities.

Noel (2003) believes that a personal inner-transformation must occur for her students before they can attempt to develop the multicultural perspective necessary for social change work. This type of pedagogy in Art education and the political nature of empowerment that this pedagogy offers is a significant contribution of Noel's work. To aid her students' personal transformation, readings and art projects were assigned, and rather than being asked to complete research papers, her students' final project was a public art exhibition "representing their new understandings of social justice" (p. 16). The students' reflective writing supported the exhibition.

As a result of her students' work and learning in her course, Noel (2003) identified three key components to her approach that allowed the "creation of artwork to move students toward a socially transformative perspective on teaching" (p. 16). These included:

being inspired or angered by a reading, discussion, or event,

overcoming invisibility, finding personal modes of expression, and

understanding the depth and complexity of social justice issues. (pp. 16-17)

Noel witnessed her students moving from their personal identity explorations and efforts, to understanding justice issues, to becoming socially transformative educators within their own classrooms, or, as she says, quoting Billings (1995) (as cited in Noel, 2003), moving from "the artist's personal experience of aesthetics to [the] development of an ethical point of view" (p. 22).

The model and methods Noel (2003) employs provide a cogent, critical, multicultural pedagogy to use for art teacher educators with social justice education as their priority. My hope is that my research will add bulk to arts-based pedagogies of this kind and encourage their implementation not only for Art teacher education, but for social justice teacher education in particular and *all* of teacher education in general.

Arts-based Teacher Education and the Arts and Social Justice in Adult Education

Carolyn Kenny, who currently serves as Professor of Human Development and Indigenous Studies at Antioch University's Ph.D. in Leadership and Change doctoral program and also served as my dissertation chair, presents a groundbreaking model of arts-based teacher education. Kenny (1998), in *A Sense of Art: A First Nations View,* employs arts-based pedagogy, reclaiming traditional native culture, worldview, and practices in her work in First Nation teacher education. Drawing from the wisdom inherent in her culture, Kenny believes *knowledge* is expressed potently "through ceremonies, rich in arts such as song, dance, [and] mask" (p. 77). As seen in Noel's (2003) work, the exploration of identity *through the arts* plays a key role in Kenny's program, and, through that exploration, a sense of community results. "In our poems, our art, our dance," says Kenny, "we reveal ourselves to one another and to society at large" (p. 78).

The power of creativity, the development of qualitative sensibilities—or what Kenny (1998) calls "the sense of art" (p. 77)—and knowledge of the land are the essential components employed to prepare students to teach with an Aboriginal perspective. "We encourage the sense of art in all areas," Kenny says, quoting an elder, "with a drum in one hand and a computer in the other" (p. 80). In addition to these components, other themes central to this extraordinary teacher education program encompass the arts and social change; aesthetic preference and moral development; the function of aesthetic arrest; the relationships between nature, arts, and culture; the power of creativity and imagination; performance as ritual; performance as healing; and the simple act of beholding.

"Much of our pedagogy is composed of experiences on the land," Kenny (1998) says, "we go on to the land and listen and write poetry" (p. 80). This is a living, healing pedagogy that fosters empathy and one that "weaves itself together in a context of real life experiences with each other and in our communities" (p. 81). Through this arts-based teacher education program, Kenny returns to her students the vital gift of their wisdom culture to bring to bear in their own teaching. Her rich pedagogical practice is aimed at recollecting cultural wisdom practices and reclaiming, reminding, and re-teaching students to use them in their teaching practice to revivify and teach using their culture's ancient wisdom in modern times, where it is just as much needed, perhaps even more so, than in the past.

As a teacher educator, I connect not only with the pedagogical practices of performance as ritual, arts, and identity; arts as inquiry tool; and arts and community building (to name just a few), that Kenny (1998) sets forth, but, I also appreciate and strive to emulate the methods Kenny employed for documenting the process of developing and teaching such practices, so that others may draw inspiration from the methods used to develop and chronicle their own teacher education work. Although developed for First Nation teachers, I believe this wisdom culture pedagogy for social justice education has much to offer to the field of arts-based teacher education for social justice.

Shapiro (2004, 2006) is a pioneer in arts-based pedagogy for social justice. Her initial research, upon which her doctoral dissertation was based, was with women educational leaders; however, she has a long history in the professional development of teachers as well. As I revisited Shapiro's (2004) writing for this literature review, her imaginary help wanted ad for a new principal caught my eye. It starts out conventionally enough, but listen as she reveals her revolutionary vision of leadership:

Seeking Administrator

Proven educational leader to apply:

Ability to enhance the district's vision and strategic plan

Excellent management skills

A systems approach to organizational leadership

A proven record of aesthetic and feminist leadership

Team building through visual journaling

Time and space opener

Basket weaver

Soul weaver

Hands dirty with clay (p. 264)

By using personal identity exploration as a starting point in her research, Shapiro (2006) engaged the educational leaders with whom she worked in artmaking, followed with the exploration of their professional identity. Using "artmaking as a form of inquiry into their own experiences as educational leaders" (p. 74), Shapiro encouraged the leaders to view themselves as "arts-based researchers inquiring into social justice issues in their schools" (p. 74).

Examining their experiences as administrators *through the arts* was the starting place for catharsis and transformation, but not the end point. Shapiro (2006) says that her goal was not "for women to achieve catharsis as an end state of calm without leading to action" (p. 174). Thus, Shaprio designed "artmaking [activities] as a means for the women to interrogate their work context [and] their day-to-day experiences as women in educational leadership" (p. 178), including interactions, assumptions, power relations, and contradictions.

The artmaking activities Shapiro (2006) employed included poetry and creative nonfiction writing, centering on a time when they were aware of being *the other* and, *working from subjective perspectives*. Shapiro reported that, through artmaking, the leaders came to understand and achieve more balanced power relations in their own schools. It was through the actual artmaking processes that alternative possibilities for action emerged. "Through the artmaking," Shapiro said, "the women were able to integrate mind, body, and spirit in such a way that it seemed to help them develop their courage to act in the face of injustice" (p. 177).

As these leaders moved from the personal to the professional, so, too, did they move from their newly found artist selves to their leader selves and *through the arts* were able to combine the two. Rather than their artistic selves continuing to be separate from their administrator selves, the women were beginning to see how they might become better integrated, and, therefore, empower themselves as leaders for social justice.

The work of becoming artist leaders for these administrators was not easy. It involved the courage and willingness to examine, question, and expose their personal and professional lives, values, and assumptions. This process (aided or perhaps instigated by the arts), by necessity, involved getting in touch and working with their emotions—that tricky, sticky realm that administrators have been advised to avoid at all costs.

A discussion of Shapiro's work would not be complete without a discussion about her rationale for linking emotion and leadership for social justice through artmaking. From Shapiro's (2006) perspective, educational leadership is "a highly emotional endeavor. It evokes a range of emotions—hurt, fear, joy, anxiety, frustration, elation, shock, and others" (p. 234). Rather than exiling emotion, Shapiro advocates for its expression and for the critical function it serves as valid form of opposition, and of locating the source of its repression as a strategy to maintain dominant power.

> Conceptions and practices of leadership that idealize . . . rationality, control, and harmony tend to favor dominant groups (White, male, middle, and upper class) in schools. Voices of marginalized groups are often discounted as being angry and as the source of the school's problems, rather than as an expression of discontent that needs to be heard. (pp. 235-236)

For Shapiro, artmaking provides educational leaders with a process *and a context* for working with their emotions, laying them bare through expression, to motivate, empower, and move us passionately to action for change. As a body of work, the critical art pedagogy Shapiro has developed is indeed rare in the field of educational administration, but one that surely beckons to be utilized by teacher educators and leadership development programs interested in a living pedagogy for social justice. Privileged, as I was, to work with her as she conducted her research, I continue to be endlessly inspired and motivated by it and attribute the foundations of my own work on *palpable pedagogy* to that influence.

Current developments in adult and community education have much to offer to the field of art and social justice education. For anyone who still wonders if and how the arts might be used for social justice education, Clover and Stalker (2007) have compiled a group of essays that present examples from different parts of the world including Europe, Australia, Ukraine, and America, where the arts are being used for adult continuing education and community education for social justice. Several themes emerge as I read these essays and they are directly related to the scope of my paper. These themes include the emancipatory potential of the arts, the power of the arts to build community, the role of the arts for teaching and learning, and the ability of the arts to disrupt our logically driven thinking, bestowing on the arts their effectiveness as oppositional tools. It is the examples of the real-world use of the arts as tools of resistance and a means to direct action, alternative, and change that makes the essays presented in this collection so compelling.

The range of issues addressed, the creative forms used to address them, and the flow between theory and practice the contributing authors demonstrate are awe-inspiring to me as an arts-based social justice educator. From rebel clowning to disrupt passivity, to poetry, graffiti, theatre, quilting, and community choir at the service of leadership development in gay and lesbian youth, to political action and cultural democracy—each of these examples of adult education for social justice through the arts are works of art in themselves.

In their chapter exploring music as a form of knowledge and educational tool in the context of national and international community choirs, Albergato-Muterspaw and Fenwick (2007), wonder about "why music may not be so well recognized in promoting social justice as other arts" (p. 154). The power that song has lent to social movements, the authors say evoking Dylan, Baez, Seeger, and more currently, Live-Aid concerts, testify to the ability of song to raise awareness, change consciousness, and motivate change. It is this power that the authors believe community choir can claim in both the music and the message they choose to make.

In each of their examples, musical focus emphasizes different purposes of social justice. For instance, in the Syracuse Community Choir:

> The meaning of diversity in community is continually fore-grounded through
> deliberate inclusion of differently-abled members who might normally be

excluded from a performing choir. The choral requirement of close listening to one another and achieving collective harmony demands an intimacy that forces people to confront and work through tensions of difference at very personal levels. (Albergato-Muterspaw & Fenwick, 2007, p. 158)

Making and communicating meaning through song aligns the multiple levels of our human makeup. The "merging of one's breathing with the rhythms and arc of a musical phrase, of virtually taking the tune simultaneously into one's lungs and ears, is an experience that weds spirit, body, emotion, and imagination" (Albergato-Muterspaw & Fenwick, 2007, p. 161) at the service of social justice.

In the next and final section of this review, I will continue to explore the dimensions of beauty and reveal its ability to wed spirit, body, emotion, and imagination in leaders in the way song does in community.

Aesthetic Leadership

What do aesthetics have to do with leadership? How is beauty interpreted in its connection to leading? Hansen et al. (2007) discuss the aesthetics of leadership and by aesthetics they "refer to sensory knowledge and felt meaning" (p. 545), or meaning constructed based on "feelings about what we experience via our senses," as opposed to the meanings "we can deduce in the absence of experience, such as [through] mathematics or other realist ways of knowing" (p. 545). Eisner (2002a) concurs, and says that aesthetic experience is "a form of life pervaded by feeling" and involves "consulting one's somatic experience" (p. 231). Both argue that "knowledge is as much about feelings as cognition" (Hansen et al., 2007, p. 545). "Aesthetic knowledge," then, is fused with "sensuous perception *in the body* [italics added]" (p. 545).

Embodied, tacit, knowing, for Hansen et al. (2007), "corresponds roughly to sensory/aesthetic knowing" (p. 546). Acceptance of this correspondence would put the spotlight on a whole realm of unexplored dimensions to leadership and connect it very much to the processes that the arts instigate. Like Shapiro (2004, 2006), Hansen et al. present an epistemological argument for "aesthetic inquiry as the way to get at experience" (2007, p. 547) that would provide leaders and followers with understandings not possible through other forms of inquiry. Feeling and emotion, in this paradigm, become central to the aesthetics of leading. Aesthetic intelligence becomes an important tool for assessing one's own critical functions as a leader, of the organization, and of its members.

49

Hansen et al. (2007) call for further research to shed light on the dynamics of "emotions in transformational leadership, such as how emotions relate to feelings and inspiration regarding change" (p. 551). Again, Shapiro's (2004) research in this very area revealed a direct correlation between the two, yet little attention is given to this essential aspect of leadership and change and its potential. "The aesthetic world-view," say the authors, "seeks to open up possibilities and widen understanding of leadership by becoming knowledgeable about hidden and unrecognized sensuous ways of knowing" (Hansen et al., 2007, p. 553). I would consider this a cause for celebration, if not validation, for educators and leaders using the arts for social change education.

Unlike Hansen et al. (2007), who believe leaders manage meaning, Ladkin (2008) sees leaders more as mediators of meaning and leading as a relational phenomenon. Instead of looking exclusively at the behaviors of leaders, as most of the leadership cannon does, Ladkin is keenly interested in "the way in which these behaviors are enacted through the lens of aesthetic perception" (p. 31). Ladkin, like Scarry (1999), recognizes beauty's relation to eternal truth and its consequential banishment in modern times.

"Beauty," Ladkin says, "is one of the most repressed and taboo concepts in our secularized and materialistic times" (2008, p. 32). Ladkin examines the leadership skills of purpose, coherence, and mastery (of what is ethically good and beautiful) and proposes that the alignment and fit between these manifestations and the way in which they are embodied is the key to "how leading beautifully is created" (p. 35). For leading to be beautiful, Ladkin argues, "it must be in the aid of the best of human purposes" (p. 37).

I am ending this literature review where I began. That is, with the connection between (*and the power of*) beauty, truth, and justice. Ladkin (2008), reminiscent of Scarry (1999), articulates the context and purpose of leading beautifully in this way:

> Though rarely written about, leading beautifully has occurred as long as human beings have been acting together to create our communities, institutions, and culture. By bringing this qualitative aspect of leading to the fore, it is hoped that both leaders and those who follow them might become more attentive to beauty, as well as other aesthetic responses, and value those responses for the sensory, spiritual and moral knowledge with which they are invested. (p. 40)

Clearly, Ladkin's (2008) call for an attention to beauty *and* the moral knowledge in which it is invested is a leitmotif within the existing one, or a theme within a theme. As stated earlier, the recurring leitmotif of this paper is the epistemology of aesthetics. The theme within that leitmotif, voiced by the multiple theorists quoted herein and central to this paper, is the *moral imperative* that beauty and the arts compel in us.

I have brought together unique strands from several disciplines to this literature review to argue for the use of the arts as a humanizing and catalyzing pedagogy for social justice teacher education. These interrelated strands, framed within the epistemology of aesthetics, the leitmotif of this paper, included: the roots of art, beauty, justice, and humanity; aesthetic education, critical theory, and humanistic education; multicultural art teacher education; arts-based teacher education; the arts and social justice in adult and community education; and aesthetic leadership. It is my hope that the dazzling array of thinking and knowing revealed through the literature discussed here impresses the reader and makes beautifully the case for continued synthesis of these strands and further research to build upon their merits and sustain the argument for the expansion of knowledge through the arts.

Chapter III: Research Methodology

As we have seen in chapter 2, the foundation for *palpable pedagogy* has a rich and deep historical tradition. In this chapter, I will continue to explore the epistemology of aesthetics as it relates to research methodology and in this context, I will position myself in the philosophy and theory of research methodology. Next, I will describe what methods I will use in my study and why these methods are best suited. In closing, I will describe my research process, participant selection, and ethical issues related to the study and use of the methods employed in my study.

Philosophy and Theory of the Arts as Inquiry Tool

In his unique interpretation of the philosophy of hermeneutics, Gadamer et al. (2004) prompts us to examine, interpret, and understand existence (and indeed our own situation) *in* culture and history, and posits that this kind of interpretation and understanding is inextricably bound to *context*. In chapter 2, I articulated the rich history and culture from which I, as an artist and scholar, spring—a history that connects beauty with truth, and the arts and the imagination, and the possibilities they engender, with the moral imperative to work for justice in the world. My *position* (context) as a researcher, or seeker of truth, understanding, and knowing, in the context of this book, is multilayered.

On one hand, as an artist, one of my goals is to make the explicit implicit. I am a painter and when I see a tree explicitly before me, my brush, my eyes, the colors on my pallet, the atmosphere, and the feelings stirring within me combine and take shape on my canvas, giving my implicit interpretation its own shape. On the other hand, as a researcher and scholar, one of my goals is to make the implicit explicit. As a researcher, I am infinitely interested in what factors contribute to the transformation of classrooms and what goes on implicitly in them that transforms them into *learning communities*, and to discover and reveal what goes on and makes that known or explicit. As an *artist researcher*, my goal is to combine these two discreet goals and achieve the latter with the assistance of the former.

In my mind's eye, I see these goals as two rails running towards the horizon line where they meet to become one. But then I think, "Could not this metaphor be construed as just an illusion, a trick of the trade, an artist's device to render space, a personal perspective . . . a deception?" Searching for another visual metaphor to validate my goal and role as an artist researcher, I reimagine it. I imagine the two rails again, with the goal of the artist on one and the goal of the researcher on the other. I see them on a strip running side by side. I take that strip and give it a simple twist and connect the ends. With this gesture, it has become a Mobius strip. The two separate tracks are now intersecting one another, producing infinite possibilities for the artist, the scholar, and humanity.

As an artist researcher, I am acutely familiar through my own experience of what Gadamer et al. (2004) means when they say that

> The fact that through a work of art a truth is experienced that we cannot attain in any other way constitutes the philosophic importance of art, which asserts itself against all attempts to rationalize it away. Hence, together with the experience of philosophy, the experience of art is the most insistent admonition to scientific consciousness to acknowledge its own limits. (pp. xxi-xxii)

I am aware that the very fact that I am conducting research which relies on an arts-based approach, places me tacitly in the battle of representation between the positivist, scientific, objective, quantitative paradigm on one side, and the constructivist, phenomenological, subjective, qualitative paradigm on the other. It is not my intention in this chapter to defend one or the other, but, simply to present a rationale for my methodological choice and its elegance and efficacy to best facilitate understanding, reveal truth, and expand knowledge based on the *context* and the phenomena being studied.

Arts-based research is a potent form of empirical inquiry and well-suited to educational contexts because it takes multiple perspectives into account, including those of the researcher, as well as those whose experiences are being researched. Additionally, what is felt, sensed, and experienced, rather than being dismissed as too subjective to be relied on as data, deepen and expand understanding. Empirical inquiry, says Schwandt (1997), "deals with the data of experience. Its claims are based on the evidence of observations, both those of the inquirer and the reports of people studied, that rely on the senses" (p. 36). We have already seen the importance of the senses in creating and experiencing the arts. When using the arts in research, the senses, too, are tapped to provide a rich source of data—data capable of describing tactile, visual, aural, and sensorial experiences.

In the simplest terms possible, Barone and Eisner (1997) give clarification about arts-based research as it is used in educational research: "What does it mean to say that an approach to educational research is arts-based? Arts-based is defined by the presence of certain aesthetic qualities or design elements that infuse the inquiry and its

53

writing" (p. 73). This kind of arts-based, human science research is what I employ in my study—the infusion of the aesthetic to understand and demonstrate that understanding.

In my view, arts-based research is humanistic because it allows me to focus aesthetically on my students as *people* and on their unique *lived experience* (Van Manen, 1990). I do not view my students as the subjects of my research. Both Van Manen (1990) and Bentz and Shapiro (1998) respectively frame research as caring and mindful acts. It follows then, that to conduct phenomenological research, the aesthetic dimension of human experience cannot be left out, neither from the researcher's intention and approach, nor from its impact on the students involved in the research. As we have seen in the previous chapter, this is true especially in light of the arts' connection to the humanizing aspects it sustains and the moral imperative it provokes.

Cole and Knowles (2008) echo this aspect of the moral and good in arts-informed research. "Arts informed research," they reason, "has both a clear *intellectual purpose* and *moral purpose*" (p. 66). The thorough array of qualities offered by arts-informed research that Cole and Knowles outline stress that "sound and rigorous arts-informed work has both . . . *theoretical potential* and *transformative potential*" (p. 67) The need for the researcher's clear intentionality, transparency, and reflexivity is also emphasized: "In arts-informed research, the researcher is present through an explicit *reflexive self-accounting*; her presence is also implied and *felt*, and the research text . . . clearly bears the *signature* or *fingerprint* of researcher-as-artist" (p. 65). For me, Cole and Knowles set the standard for arts-based research. They argue for the construction of knowledge that is *aesthetically* generated as a communicative and holistic process: "The central purpose of arts-informed research is knowledge advancement through research, not the production of fine artworks . . . reflecting a methodological commitment through evidence of a *principled process*, *procedural harmony*, and attention to *aesthetic quality*" (p. 65).

Additionally, Cole and Knowles (2008) posit that the arts have the potential to make scholarship more accessible to everyday people and not simply the protected commodity of a select few. "Arts-informed research maximizes its communicative potential and addresses concerns about the *accessibility* of the research account usually through the form and language in which it is written, performed, or otherwise presented" (p. 66).

54

Finally, for Cole and Knowles (2008), it is the unique contributions the arts make to the advancement of knowledge that set it apart and in contrast to more standard scientific forms of inquiry. "The knowledge advanced in arts-informed research is generative rather than propositional . . . reflecting the multidimensional, complex, dynamic, intersubjective, and contextual nature of human experience" (p. 67).

Eisner (2008) picks up on the noble strand the arts contribute to the practice of research. That is, their ability to join theory with praxis *through empathy*. "The arts address the qualitative nuances of situation . . . evoking empathy—images rendered in artistically expressive form and often generate a kind of empathy that makes action possible" (p. 10). Eisner says that the arts, in the service of research, contribute significantly to the pursuit of knowledge and understanding and "provide new ways with which to perceive and interpret the world . . . making vivid, realities that would otherwise go unknown" (p. 11).

It is the reality of my students' lived experience that I strive to understand and I am convinced that the most effective method I have at my disposal to do this is arts-based. Because my students' art-making (to inquire about, expose, and address social justice issues in their schools) is an integral aspect of what I am researching, it naturally flows, according to McNiff (1998), that art then be the tool to study this phenomenon.

McNiff (1998) encouraged researchers to utilize the arts *to inquire about* the arts. For McNiff, there is no better way to study the effects of the arts than through the arts themselves. To advance this argument, he proposed that arts-based research "grows from a trust in the intelligence of the creative process and a desire for relationships with the images that emerge from it. These two focal points," he says, "are the basis for a new tradition of inquiry" (p. 37).

I am excited to be a part of this new tradition of inquiry and trust that my selection of arts-based methods are the most logical fit for the particular *content and context* of my topic of inquiry—arts-based social justice teacher education. My trust in the versatility and intelligence of the arts is so deep that I employ the arts not only as a *pedagogical tool* to teach social justice but, also, as a *research tool* to question how this teaching is experienced by my students (and me), and to understand and highlight the contributions the arts have to offer both these functions. I believe in the power of art to speak for itself about the topic under study. As a researcher, I am at the service of understanding and knowledge, and in this service, the arts are my allies.

Ethnographic/Autoethnographic Methods

I have already examined the role of the arts as research tools and why I have chosen to use them for my inquiry. I would now like to turn to my companion method, ethnography, and examine its features as a research method and argue for its blending with the arts-based approach and its utilization as an inquiry tool in my research.

With its roots in anthropology, what distinguishes ethnography as a qualitative form of inquiry, says Schwandt (1997) is the "fact that it is the process and product of describing and interpreting *cultural* behavior" (p. 44). What is the process and what is the product to which Schwandt refers? The process is how one comes to know a culture. This is done primarily through *fieldwork* whose characteristics include: " . . . prolonged time in the *field*, generation of descriptive data, development of rapport and empathy with respondents, the use of multiple data sources, the making of *fieldnotes*, and so forth" (p. 44). The product, according to Schwandt, is how the culture is portrayed. Traditionally, this is accomplished through written text.

In both respects, the research process and product, my research is ethnographic. My process involved prolonged time in the field and focused on knowing the culture of my students through participant observation data collection in the field. My product is accomplished, not only in written text as in traditional forms of ethnography, but, also in *writing the culture* through the arts of the culture: its poetry, mask-making, multi-media autobiography, collage, drama, sound/song/music, and image making of all kinds, produced *by that culture*. The product or writing the culture I employ, in the arts-based ethnographic approach I use, is not limited to the presentation of the culture through text alone, but utilizes that culture's arts as text, as narrative, and as art that speaks for itself.

In *Researching Teaching: Exploring Teacher Development Through Reflexive Inquiry*, Cole and Knowles (2000) liken teaching to autobiography and the researching of teaching to the researching of the self for reflexive inquiry. For these authors, not only is teaching an "autobiographical act" (p. 22) that allows researchers to examine their practice over time, but they posit that "teaching *is* autobiography" (p. 22), and connect teaching, reflection, and reflexivity:

> To be a teacher is to commit to ongoing autobiographical acts (which are viewed and experienced by others). Teaching acts represent articulations of a life work in progress. Strung together, like beads on a string, the day-to-day teaching events become episodic evidence of changing perspectives and a

56

growing life in relation to society and the world at large. To teach is to be involved in lifelong reflective inquiry. (p. 22)

One of my goals as an artist researcher is reflexivity, or the ability to ask myself questions about my motivations for teaching and learning—also, to ask myself critical questions about the nature of research and why I feel it is important to be as present *in* the research as I am in teaching. In my research, I want to examine the culture, not only from my students' point of view, but from my own, as teacher attempting to teach social justice, as well. As an artist researcher, I see myself as a part of the culture, not separate and objective, without hopes and dreams within that culture. Through the documentation of my experiences, I want to chronicle not only my students' processes of experience, discovery, and learning, but also my own and welcome my experience to be viewed and experienced by others. Through my own art processes, I become transparent and reflective as a researcher, teacher, and co-creator of the culture I am simultaneously seeking to understand. I experience this as an autoethnographic process (study of self as culture), and believe the revelation/self-revelation gained in the process has much to offer students and teachers of social justice alike.

In this chapter, I have articulated the philosophy and theory grounding arts-informed research because it is an essential component of the methods that I will employ in my research. As a practitioner-researcher, I experience and utilize methodology as multi-dimensional and layered as the phenomena at the center of my inquiry. My research approach to the study of the classroom culture generated when the arts are used as pedagogical tools for social justice teacher education is best described as ethnographic/autoethnographic. In the tradition of classic ethnographic study, I strive to recognize the "intrinsic, indigenous principles of order and organization that permeate social forms—discursive, visual, and material . . . " (Atkinson, 2005, p. 1).

What is unique in my research approach is that I am inviting the arts to assist me in recognizing, understanding, and interpreting these ethnographic forms. Indeed, I believe that an arts-based ethnographic approach is a poignantly apt one and will provide me with the type of kaleidoscopic vision necessary to adequately explore the complex regions of culture in an arts-based social justice teacher education course.

Research Process and Participant Selection

In 2005, I was asked by the chair of the Humanistic/Multicultural Education graduate program at the State University of New York, where I have served as an adjunct instructor for the last 13 years, to write a new course for the program. Having written a course, for the same program called "Expressive Arts in Education and Human Services," which I taught for 13 years (along with a myriad of other courses in multicultural education, special education, and elementary courses), I felt equal to the task. The first course I wrote focused on the healing power of the arts in the human services *and* their function as social/emotional literacy tools to support affective education.

As a Ph.D. in Leadership and Change student, I saw this invitation as an opportunity to write a new course that could create a new context for the expressive arts/arts that would capitalize on and channel the power of the arts in the service of leadership and change. I taught the resulting teacher education course, "Expressive Arts, Leadership, and Change," for three consecutive years (2006, 2007, and 2008) (see Appendix A for composite syllabus).

This three-credit graduate course was taught in a compressed summer session, consisting of 40 instructional hours, chunked out in 5 full days spanning 4 weeks between July and August, with a three-hour introductory evening class at the beginning of the session. The first summer I taught the course was 2006 and I used it as the topic of my first independent learning agreement for my doctoral program and titled it "*Palpable Pedagogy*: Using the Arts to Teach Social Justice Pedagogy." My focus during this first year was three-fold. I focused on the actual *content* of the course, (what I was going to teach), the *methods* (how I would go about teaching it), and the *culture* (what kind of culture was created when content and methods included the arts).

In the summer of 2007, I taught the course, "Expressive Arts, Leadership, and Change," for the second time, and again it served as the topic for my second independent learning agreement, which was titled "An Ethnographic Study of Classroom Culture in an Arts-Based Social Justice Teacher Education Course." My focus during the second year was to be primarily a continuation of the study of culture I had begun the year before. I planned to more consciously undertake the application of arts-based research methods in my study of culture. The first year, I had done this unconsciously, as the material implored me to let it speak for itself.

In the summer of 2008, I taught the course for a third time. My focus during the third year was to continue the study of culture. Also, because I had noticed over the last two years that as emotional realms were exposed through the arts, *fear* of art, as a subtext or antenarrative (Boje, 2001), emerged, begging to be explored, I decided to continue the study of culture for the third year, with the intention of exploring fear as a phenomenon. The result of this sustained multi-year focus on understanding the culture engendered in an arts-based social justice teacher education course was a very large data set, spanning three consecutive years and a wealth of ethnographic material with which to understand the culture and life worlds of my students and myself, and hopefully to shed light on the effects of the arts on teaching and learning for social justice.

Additionally, as indicated in the preceding section, in addition to the collection of information of and about my students' experiences, I documented my own process as a social justice teacher educator using the arts to teach social justice. I examined my process in autoethnographic fashion through personal reflection, art-making, reflective journaling, with attention to reflexivity through the arts. In a very real sense, I was "researching teaching through researching myself" (Cole & Knowles, 2000, p. 25).

Ethical Considerations

In 2006, I obtained IRB approval from Antioch University to conduct research. The following year, in 2007, I updated my application to continue to collect data and to conduct interviews with students *after* their grades were submitted, reasoning that I might capture a clearer, more frank and open assessment of their experience. This extension was granted and, in the fall of 2007, the interviews commenced. In 2008, I submitted a request for an extension of my approval to do research for this final round of teaching "Expressive Arts, Leadership, and Change."

In 2006, 12 students enrolled for my course. After the first session, 2 dropped the course citing scheduling conflicts, which left 10 students enrolled and all of these chose to sign informed consents and participate in my research. In 2007, 16 students were enrolled in my course; of those, 15 chose to participate and 1 student declined. In 2008, 11 students enrolled in the course; of those, 10 chose to participate, and 1 declined. Participation in my research, as stated in the informed consent, was strictly voluntary.

I made a commitment to my students that I would not ask them to participate in anything that I would not do myself. This included suggested exercises, required assignments, or reciprocal sharing of highly charged feelings through debriefings and dialogues. I was still keenly aware of the significant ethical considerations involved when the teacher has the double role of teacher/researcher. Because of the fundamental power differential inherent in the teacher/student dyad alone, it warranted my careful, conscious consideration.

From the outset, I developed safeguards against conflicts of interest, including verbal and written explanations of the purpose of my study and detailed informed consent forms, each emphasizing student participation as optional. Additionally, I invited my students to view themselves as co-researchers and participate in the process of discovery along with me, as well as sharing openly my personal, autoethnographic processes. All of my students who opted to participate in my study seized upon this invitation. Indeed, even my students who declined to participate formally in the study participated fully in all aspects of the course. With few exceptions, my students expressed wild excitement about the processes to which they were introduced in the class, their personal journeys of growth and learning, and for those who did chose to participate, the contribution to the field that their participation in the study would allow.

Summary

Because of the progressive nature of this ethnographic study, I was able to capture a treasure load of data, revealing multi-layered aspects of an arts-based social justice teacher education course and the culture it fostered. I gathered detailed information over a three-year period in the form of classroom artifacts such as student journal entries, art-making, artwork, assignments, dialogues, impressions, presentations, collaborations, exhibitions, interviews, artist statements, and burning questions, via participant observation field notes, teaching journal, photographs, audio recordings, video recordings, formal interviews, informal feedback sessions, and formal and informal course evaluations.

These data, including the running record of my impressions and analysis along the way, provided me with substantial evidence of a sustained and lengthy study of the culture as it developed over time—culminating in, what Geertz (1983) refers to as a thick description of that culture and a massive, dazzling data pool to be catalogued, reviewed, and interpreted. The two independent learning agreements produced during the course of this study, testify to my ability to conduct arts-based ethnographic research that has a strong potential of making a significant contribution to the fields of social justice teacher education, Art education, and leadership and change studies.

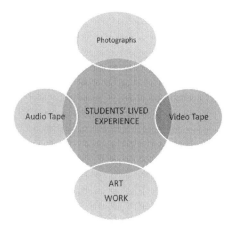

Figure 3.1. The data streams.

In chapter 4, I will review the data I collected, catalogued, and sorted, using classroom artifacts to assist me in *writing culture*. I will select, analyze, interpret, and present these data sets (representing my students' experience and my own) allowing the reader to enter the *life worlds* of my students, myself, and the culture that was manifested to understand better the critical function of the arts, as a *palpable pedagogy* for social justice teacher education.

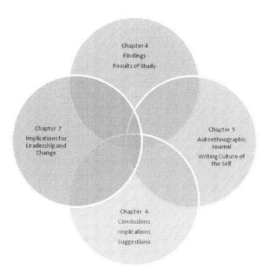

Figure 3.2. What each of the following chapters will address.

Chapter 5 will contain my Autoethnographic journal, a three-year chronicle of my discovery of the *wisdom* culture of myself. In chapter 6, I will discuss my conclusions, implications of the study, and my suggestions for future research. In chapter 7, my final chapter, I will discuss the implications of this research for leadership and change.

Chapter IV: Findings and Results of Study

Introduction

Over three consecutive summers, from 2006 to 2008, I taught a graduate course called "Expressive Arts, Leadership, and Change," at a state college in upstate New York. The course was offered as an elective in a social justice teacher education program. In the first year of the course, 10 students participated, 16 students the second year, and 11 in the third, totaling 37 students in all. Of these 37 students, only 2 chose not to participate in this study (1 in 2007, and 1 in 2008). As an artist-researcher/educator, my goal was to understand the unique classroom culture that emerged when an *arts-based* approach to social justice teacher education was employed. The methods I used included an arts-informed ethnographic/autoethnographic inquiry approach, and collected data over the three-year period.

These qualitative data include photographs, video and audio tape of classroom events, as well as my students' journal entries, photographs of their expressive artwork, their homework assignments, their final papers, and face-to-face interviews I conducted with five students in the fall of 2007 (two 2006 and three 2007 students). Additionally, my own direct participant observation of my students' interactions, activities, and responses to the course content, processes, environment, and learning recorded in my teaching journal (and my own personal autoethnographic journal) round out my data pool.

Recorded student interviews (see Appendix B for interview questions), conducted in September and October of 2007, assisted me in understanding the culture, from my *students'* point of view. For students that could not meet with me face-to-face, but were willing to answer my interview questions, I supplied a copy of my interview guide and welcomed them to respond to the questions in writing. In all, 10 students submitted written responses to my interview questions. All students were given pseudonyms to protect their identity and maintain confidentiality. As already indicated, I developed an autoethnographic study, meaning a study of the culture of *self* as a college professor using the arts to teach social justice in a teacher education course, to support my self-reflexive process as an artist-educator/researcher. This autoethnography chronicles my personal and professional impressions, realizations, and epiphanies—balancing as an ethnographer, "the conflicting demands of a performance in which the identity of the self as well as the 'other' are jointly explored" (Humphreys, Brown, & Hatch, 2003, p. 10).

The themes that emerged from the data were gleaned after repeated review of and emersion in the data outlined above, until saturation was reached. I used a simple, low-tech method of color-coding as I reviewed the multiple sources of data to identify recurring themes and track the details of patterns and sub-themes. Frequency of theme was considered as I blended data and narrowed down the themes; but richness of revelation of significant aspects of the culture was given equal consideration, as I selected the themes on which to report, hoping to expose both the breadth and depth of the data.

These themes will be elucidated through student experiences manifested through their assignments, journal entries, poetry, and visual artwork. I will report on these, shedding light on the culture through narrative text and visuals, including photos of students and their work, and graphic models to help organize and make sense of the data. At times, I will focus on a particular student for narrative cohesion and especially because that student represents the vast experiences of many. Students' pseudonyms will be followed by a year to indicate the year that student took the course (i.e., Alan, 2008 class). However, because students visited subsequent classes after taking the class and interviews were conducted in 2007, the *same* student may have differing or multiple year citations associated with quotes attributed to her or him.

By employing multiple modes of collecting and representing the information I collected, it is my hope that readers will glean meaning from and understanding of the culture through their own active imagination, as well as through mine. Thomas (2004), whose chapter in the book *Provoked by Art: Theorizing Arts-informed Research*, entices me, as a researcher, to find meaning in my power of perception and allow meaning to form through the images reflecting the multiple dimensions (represented through the data) of the culture I collected and through the feelings (as a way of knowing) they engender:

> Images absorb knowledge, may saturate the reader, and are dripping with meaning. Visual representations are not transfixed; there are no limits to their capacity for luminosity, their capacity for meaning. Meanings embedded in visual imagery are illuminated as the reader becomes immersed in aesthetic descriptions and fuse the intellectual realm of ideas with the sensual realm of flesh. A chasm narrows between artist/researcher and the artwork;

artist/researcher and the reader; reader and the aesthetic hermeneutical forms through acts of perception and altering meanings. (p. 67)

I feel a sense of liberation in knowing that my cognitive ability to reason and make meaning of (both mine and my students') experiences is supported by my ability to sense, feel, and make meaning through images, impressions, and feeling—bringing the mind, body, and heart to bear in my interpretation. In a sense, I have tripled my capacity as an artist-educator/researcher by joining mind (reason/intellect/imagination), body (sensory awareness), and heart (emotion/feeling) at the service of inquiry and knowledge. In a very real sense, I am jointly exploring mine and my students' processes in this study to shed light on the culture—treating myself in this research as explicitly "of the data" (Butler, 1997, p. 933). And finally, as an artist-ethnographer, I will "shape the ethnography, a process in which imagination and an aesthetic sense play crucial roles" (Humphreys et al., 2003, p. 10).

Figure 4.1. Student with Self-portrait Mask, 2006.

"The Arts" Defined

"The experience of art," says Dutton (1994), "is paradise regained" (p. 239). Before presenting the data, my findings, and my analysis, I would like to clarify for the reader my use of the term, *art.* I will be using art to signify all of the expressive arts, including, but not limited to visual, performing, and literary arts: including, but not limited to painting, photography, collage, sculpture, drama, song, voice, music, poetry, prose, and multi-media art forms. Additionally, my use of the arts is inclusive of art appreciation, including the viewing of, interacting with, and making meaning of works of art. Throughout this paper, the arts will refer to engagement in the creative processes (as outlined above), including encounters with and experience of making art, and the use of the arts individually and/or in tandem.

With few exceptions, the majority of my students were not artists as contemporary culture defines *artist*. However, the data show that their encounters with the arts enabled them to express themselves, reveal themselves to one another, make meaning of the course content, and inquire about issues of justice in a way that, as one student put it, went "deeper than words." In a very real sense, as will be revealed through these data, my students reclaimed the power of the arts as their human birthright (Dissanayake, 1992).

The Themes

Figure 4.2. Identified themes.

In the introduction to this paper, I discussed three of the themes that emerged as my data were reviewed. In this section, I will elaborate on these three themes: identity, reflection, and dialogue more fully as they shed light on essential elements of the culture. In addition, *community* emerged as a strong theme as I explored my students' impressions of the culture of the course more deeply.

Figure 4.3. Identified sub-themes.

Additionally, the *emotional* impact of the arts, *fear* of art, *compassion* evoked through the arts, and *action* motivated through the arts also emerged as compelling subthemes and will be thoroughly examined. I will discuss how my students experienced identity, reflection, dialogue, community, emotion, fear of art, compassion, and action. Ultimately, it is my hope to illuminate how my students' experiences contributed to the development of a unique culture in an arts-based social justice teacher education graduate course.

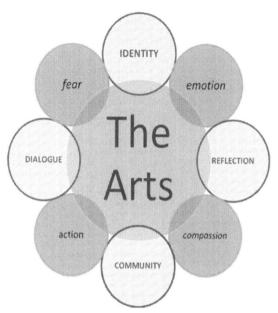

Figure 4.4. Interconnected themes and subthemes.

The themes, although distinct in some respects, are deeply interconnected. I will examine each primary theme under its own heading and frequently themes will be paired together as they organically emerged from the data. For instance, students' identity explorations and their reflection (through art-making and journaling) on these explorations were shared in dyads, in small dialogue groups, and with the larger classroom community in dialogue. The subthemes will be woven throughout the chapter, as ultimately, all of the thematic and subthematic processes are inextricably bound. Identity explorations (bringing up emotions), reflection (through the arts can bring up fear of art), dialogue (engenders compassion), and community (building and activity) inspired, motivated, and supported students as they collaboratively created action plans for social justice work in the world. The keen reader will identify these interweavings throughout the chapter.

What should stand out as the data is revealed to be unique in the context of social justice education is how my students were involved in identity exploration, reflection, dialogue, and community building and activity. Specifically, the data highlight that my students were involved in these processes not just verbally and theoretically, but dynamically and experientially through the engagement of their senses, emotions, and imaginations via the arts.

A Few Words About Beauty

In the preceding chapters of this book, I believe my fondness for beauty is evident and the reader may detect an inclination on my part to use the terms beauty and art interchangeably. I understand these terms are not synonymous and still choose to associate them with one another because, for me, they represent both a way of knowing and (my definition of) truth. Certainly, not all art is beautiful in a literal sense, but in a metaphorical sense it is beautiful—as it is representative of the particular palpable truth of the artist and a sensorial means of understanding. Hopefully, this will clarify my use of these essential terms and pique the readers' interest in following my line of reasoning, as I present my research data.

Identity: Autobiography—Past, Present, and Future

Scarry (1999), in her essay *On Beauty and Being Just*, helps frame the recursive nature of beauty in relation to time and to education. She says

> The very pliancy or elasticity of beauty—hurtling us forward and back, requiring us to break new ground, but obliging us also to bridge back not only to the ground we just left but to still earlier, even ancient, ground—is a model for the pliancy and lability of consciousness in education. (p. 46)

As a method for exploring identity, autobiography juxtaposed multiple levels of students' experience and memory to create a story, their story, my story. While teaching Expressive Arts, Leadership, and Change, I discovered that the autobiographical process allowed my students to explore the roots of social justice concerns in their own lives (past), enlighten their work in the field of education and human services (present), and assist them in making a firm commitment to their continued social justice work (future). Alan (2008 class) theorizes that the autobiographical process enhances purposefulness.

In *Releasing the Imagination: Essays on Education, the Arts, and Social Change*, Greene (1995) devotes a chapter titled, "The Shapes of Childhood Recalled," to the theme of autobiography. "We reach out into the world—touching, listening, watching what presents itself to us from our pre-reflective landscapes, primordial landscapes," she says, using landscape as a metaphor for self. "We strain toward horizons: horizons of what might be, horizons of what was" (p. 73). For Greene, the autobiographical process joins identity with reflection, urging us to connect the present with the past, and use all of our experiences as fuel to power our imagination and envision a world of alternative possibilities. Indeed, Greene (1979) sees a tangible connection between teachers' recollecting their stories and their subsequent stance on social issues.

> Looking back, recapturing their stories, teachers can recover their own standpoints on the social world. . . . Making an effort to interpret the texts of their life stories, listening to others' stories in whatever "web of relationships" they find themselves, they may be able to multiply the perspectives through which they look upon the realities of teaching; they may be able to choose themselves anew in the light of an expanded interest, an enriched sense of reality. (p. 33)

In an interview with one of my students, Don (2006 class), light was shed on the processes of identity and reflection—processes that can hardly be separated into categories, not even for organizing this paper, because ultimately the exploration of identity goes hand-in-hand with reflection. When asked about the culture as he experienced it, Don responded.

> The whole culture of the room enhanced my learning experience because I knew that I already knew a lot of what I needed to know when I walked in there and that what I was going to find out and what I needed to find out was what I needed to know about myself and others. I felt it. I sort of felt it when I started journaling. I really felt it. It was almost like the camel. You feel the weight of good things that you are carrying with you but they are not integrated at the given moment that you are just feeling the weight of them. (D.C., interview, 9-1-07, p. 5)

Don (2006 class) knew what he needed to know when he entered the class, but just needed the structure, permission, and time to reflect and dialogue about it. Like Alan, Don experienced the exploration of his identity as an integrating process. His response is representative of the feelings of many students who felt that they knew, or had within them, what they needed to learn, or relearn, or reclaim. Many students referred to journal keeping as a reflective tool that assisted them in the exploration of their identity. For Don, the course (and its culture) provided him with a way to organize what he already knew about himself in relation to social justice. His keen awareness of his own process reveals the key role that time (past, present, and future) plays in his self-exploration process. During his interview Don explains it cogently:

It was archeological. I always felt like I was acquiring the tool that I could look back at my experience with and make better sense of it. And you can turn that scope forward, too, and it can work in the present. It can work in the future and, in your class, I was in the present. I was using the past. I was using the present. I was really looking towards the future but I was in the present, which felt really good. I have often had trouble living in the present and it was nice to live in the present. I think it was helped by everybody else's experience because, I mean, there were people around me, including myself, having profound experiences in there and you could see them. You could hear it in their voices. It was breathtaking to behold. (D.C., interview, 9-1-07, p. 6)

Don's (2006 class) comments remind me of my original interest for my research topic. When my Committee Chair, Carolyn Kenny, originally inquired about my topic in 2005 at an advisory meeting in Seattle, I said that I wanted to study a *wisdom culture*, learn from that culture about how they made and negotiated *change*, and apply that wisdom knowledge in my work as a social justice educator and school principal. My intuition was that the arts somehow played a role.

In the years since that conversation, I discovered that my own culture had so much to teach me about change and, ultimately, that my own life was resplendent with the wisdom and culture of the self, so I should not be surprised then to realize that my students, too, discovered this truth for themselves. It is my turn, now, to have my breath taken away when I re-read Don's "I Am From" poem, written in couplets. Listen for the landscape, the earth, the past, present, and future, the wisdom ground and courage of this amazing student's life world.

I Am From

I am from orchards and dirt lanes
I am from sibling rival growth pains
I am from bus driver's groping
I am from middle child coping
I am from gold stars, nuns, and rulers
I am from the guild of parent foolers
I am from substance abuse
I am from out, running loose
I am from high school slumber

I am from the failing number

I am from all the same faces

I am from suburban places.

I am from where we smother the other

I am from off the ground, splash and sound

I am from turning around, I've found myself, circling

I am from being afraid

I am from getting bills paid

I am from causing pain

I am from anxiety insane

I am from wanting to stop hurting, the others

I am from the once was lost

I am from the now am found

I am from the thorny ground

I am from the new creation

I am from my heart's elation

I am from the title 'Daddy'

I am from Dear Sarah's hug

I am from the College Center

I am from the blurring years

I am from the fifties fears

I am from the Milton farm

I am from the Highland homestead

I am from the fed and warm bed

I am from firecracker summers

I am from bad acid bummers

I am from a time line elusion

I am from misplaced memories

I am from emotions freeze

I am from after baseball but before Frisbees

I am from neighborhood pickup games, everybody looked the same

I am from towering pines

I am from squealing clothes lines, wisteria vines, cheap wines

I am from Sunday sauce

I am from boulder's moss, careless loss

I am from the rage of Ralph

I am from gentle Joe

I am from the devil's paddock

I am from the host of free

I am from the high grass summer

I am from the snowy shroud

I am from the broken promise

I am from by standing crowd

(D.C., 2006)

For me, the last line of Don's poem represents a place in his journey where he stops and witnesses his life unfurled over time, with others' witnessing their lives as well. As we will see as this chapter unfolds, the process created a very strong sense of compassion and empathy for self and other, which is most certainly a prerequisite for social justice work (see Appendix C for a sample of other students' "I Am From" poems).

Patton (2007 class) also uses a temporal frame of reference (reverence) to describe his journey and the shaping of his identity over time:

> The class opened so many possibilities for me and really helped me to see so much about myself while simultaneously reminding me of the journey that has brought me to where I am now. In the chaos of the world, we seem to forget the past and want to move on to the future. However, it was my past that helped shape who I am and I must honor that. The class was a gentle reminder to honor that part of my journey and it allowed me to manifest itself into a beautiful table, and beautiful emotions, and wonderful connections with people. (P.B., written response to interview questions, 10-3-07, p. 2)

Figure 4.5. Patton's table under construction, with close-up, 2007.

The table to which Patton refers in his statement (see Figure 4.5) was inspired by our class visit to the Samuel Dorskey Museum on campus. Patton worked on it during his weeks in the course and finished it prior to the last class. Throughout the course he kept us all abreast of his progress and finally produced a photo of his finished work. Along with inspiration for the table, Patton indicates that emotion and connection resulted from his identity exploration.

It appears that the autobiographical process itself contributed to creating a culture that allowed students to recollect the threads of their life story and weave them together with the threads of their life's work as educators and recognize themselves as leaders, and reorient, refocus, and reclaim a lost part of themselves. Reclaim a part of themselves? Yes, Don, put it this way: "With the exception of the time compression, this didn't feel like work—I'm not going to say (it was like) Christmas but I've recovered a lot of self that was lost" (Barbera, Don in dialogue group, conversation fragment captured in teaching journal, 2006c, p. 25).

In the closing of her "I Am From" poem, Lindsey encapsulates how the autobiographical process acts to gather the myriad experiences of a life together as a whole to simultaneously connect with her self and with others:

I am from all that I have ever smiled, smelt, touched, noticed, appreciated or haven't. From the bottom of my foot to the tip of my hand, from the center of my heart to the many miles between me and you. Who are you from? Where are you from? I want to know. (L.O., transcribed audio recording, student retrospective show, 7-28-07, p. 1)

Figure 4.6. Lindsey's journal: "I Am From" poem, 2007.

The themes of identity and community converge with action for Maria (2007 class). She, too, affirms the power of revealing herself to herself, and herself to others. For Maria, this process morphed into action in the wider community as she incorporated it in her practice as a pedagogical tool for her teaching. This is what she said in her written feedback to my interview question about culture:

It was a wonderful environment. Not only did I learn about myself, but I learned about others as well. This gave me greater insight into the human plight, (and a process) which I am now using in my classroom at South Junior High in [Name of city]. (M.G., written response to interview, 11-07, p. 2)

Through her mask-making, Ellie (2007 class) provides a stunning example of how the exploration of identity resulted in a powerful integration of her internal and external self. Let us take a look at her mask and her accompanying Artist Statement.

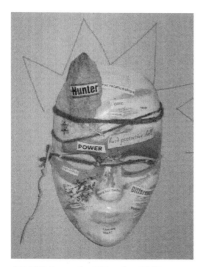

Figure 4.7. Ellie's mask of identity, 2007.

Ellie's (2007 class) artist statement follows

In creating this mask, I choose to look at (my) identity as comprised of both the external face I show the world and the internal thoughts and feelings that I may keep hidden from the world. I tried to suggest that a combining of these states would be both revealing and powerful. (E.S., artist statement, 7-27-07)

Tia (2007 class) felt identity and community combined to form a unique culture as she and her fellow students revealed themselves to each other—and through that revelation, developed a sense of community. In fact, as students explored and shared their stories, they were building trust and through this recurring reciprocal process cultivating the roots of community.

I think there was a unique classroom culture in this course. I felt that through our own similarities and differences each person in the class contributed to making our own supportive culture in the class. I felt we formed a community that was respectful, understanding, and highly supportive and helpful to all. (T.A., written response to interview, 11-07, p. 1)

The culture and climate to which Tia and Ellen refer was co-created by students willing to deeply reflect on their own identities, their past in relation to their present, and both in relation to their future. These were students who were moved by that exploration and allowed themselves to be moved by one anothers' journey. They were students who were able to review their lives in relation to change and to be changed by it. These were students, many of whom said they "could not draw a stick figure," who were willing to employ the arts (sometimes for the first time in their lives) to feel, to emote, and to recognize and honor their identity as a source of pride and strength. The following excerpt (originally from my teaching journal of 2007) reflects my admiration for my students:

This was a culture where students felt compelled to change the lens they use to see themselves and others. These changelings are future leaders, adept at empathy and compassion, able to see the past, present, and future in the present moment, able to be flexible and reflexive and will be able use their hearts to softly and firmly lead for social justice. (Barbara, independent learning project, 2007a, p. 32)

Leggo (2004), an arts-based poet researcher, joins together many of the dimensions of identity exploration that have emerged thus far in this study of the culture in this arts-based social justice class. He says

To change the self is to change how one sees the world. The past is for-giving, always present, still living, being lived, and the future is like the past, also present, the stories that return when we attend to the art and heart of story-living, no linear progression like verb tenses in grammar handbooks, heartful and artful attending in the momentous moment, the present moment, where past and future are tangled lines composing a location, a circle of earth, heart, time, life, all circles, a curriculum of eternal moments for standing firm and flexible with hopeful remembering. (p. 33)

Figure 4.8. Student points to compassion as a key element of her self-portrait, 2006.

According to my students, the exploration of identity through the autobiographical process, or the archeology of self (Pinar, 1994), was a critical component of their learning environment. Ultimately, the process evoked compassion and respect. By looking at their own lives compassionately, they were able to experience others compassionately. By recognizing their differences, they were able to recognize their similarities. By recognizing they were more alike than different, they were able to imagine how the autobiographical process might be used with their own students to foster mutual respect and how this process, taken to a universal level, might be used as a tool for social justice to foster connection and, in turn, collaborative work for change. Joan (2007 class) puts the connection between identity and action very cogently:

> I see this process (of identity exploration) as getting to know what is inside us, naming it, looking at it, examining it in light of social justice and change, and then sharing on a deep level with others to promote change. I can do this with the tools I have learned and will continue to learn. (J.B., final paper, 2007, p. 3)

I will end this section on identity (although the theme will continue directly into the next section and throughout the chapter) with an audio clip of a dialogue group in progress. Students have been reflecting on their autobiographical process and are sharing their journaled reflections with one another.

Reflection

Palmer (1998), in *Courage to Teach*, refers to the practice of reflection as a sort of inner speech resulting in deep learning.

> Words are not the sole medium of exchange in teaching and learning—we educate with silence as well. Silence gives us a chance to reflect on what we have said and heard, and silence itself can be a sort of speech, emerging from the deepest parts of ourselves, of others, of the world . . . in authentic education, silence is treated as a trustworthy matrix for the inner work students must do, a medium for learning of the deepest sort. (p. 77)

Like Palmer, Schon (1987) emphasizes the fundamental logic of reflective practice and reasons on its behalf. He posits that it is a pedagogical practice on which teachers can rely to help solve the complex issues facing schools and as an antidote to the simplistic reliance on the "technical rationality of schools' prevailing epistemology" (Spalding & Wilson, 2002, p. 1395). Indeed, says Schon, "Professional education should be

78

redesigned to combine the teaching of applied science with coaching in the artistry of reflection-in-action" (p. xii). Reflection-in-action will be the focus of this theme's exploration.

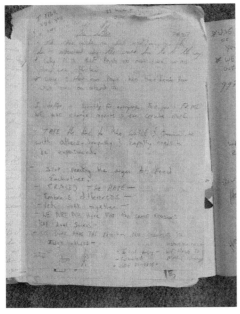

Figure 4.9. Lindsey's journal entry on "The Letter," 2007.

Initially, students reflected on their own lives and narratives. However, just as importantly, they reflected on the course content, including essential questions posed to dialogue groups related to power, oppression, and "isms" in schools, discussion of assigned readings, in and out of class, course assignments, response and reactions to classroom experiences. One such classroom experience was the viewing of the documentary film, *The Letter: An American Town and the 'Somali Invasion'* (Hamzeh, 2003) screened during class. Other experiences included students' Cultural Plunge and Cross Cultural Interviews (Katz & Ryan, 2005), and their Student Action Plans and planning process.

Figure 4.10. Lindsey's reflective journal cover, 2007.

Reflection Through Journal Writing

Students referred to having the time to reflect on their lives and course experiences as a key element of the classroom culture. Representative of this aspect was many students' appreciation of journal keeping. Ellie (2007 class) wrote:

> I appreciated that in class we were given the opportunity to journal our thoughts and feelings immediately during or following an exercise—this helped me to just do it! And I can say that at the end of this experience, I feel like I may continue to keep an expressive arts journal. (E.S., self-learning and evaluation paper, 8-3-07, p. 7)

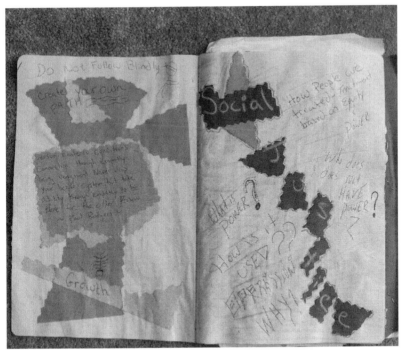

Figure 4.11. Inside Lindsey's reflective journal, 2007.

Lindsey (2007 class) referred to journaling as *journalizing*. The energy of the word journalizing helped me appreciate her process of journaling (writing and drawing in her journal), and artfully reflecting through her own unique collage process and then, it seems, reciprocally, her journaling process giving her something in return. Here are her words on her process:

> Although I have many positive things to say about this course and have enjoyed everything that we have done, journalizing has been my absolute favorite. I have learned to express myself not only through writing, but sketching as well. Reflecting and evaluating my emotions of past and present has become my healing and growing medicine. This form of expression has really opened my creative mind and I find [it's] easier for me to express myself. I take an abundance of pride in my journalizing and continue to journal everyday. (L.O., self-learning and evaluation paper, 8-4-07, p. 3)

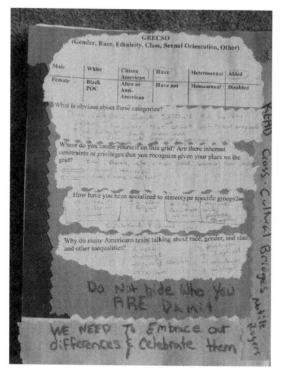

Figure 4.12. Lindsey's reflection of G.R.E.S.C.O. (Katz & Ryan, 2005).

Healing and growing medicine? The curative power of this process for Lindsey is obvious. Emotional comfort, from time immemorial, has been an attribute associated with the arts. For Ellie (2007 class), Don (2006 class), and Lindsey (2007 class), and, as we will see going forward, many others, journal keeping evolved as a practice in their personal, as well as their professional lives as teachers, equipping them with an important tool for becoming self reflective, reflection-in-action educators.

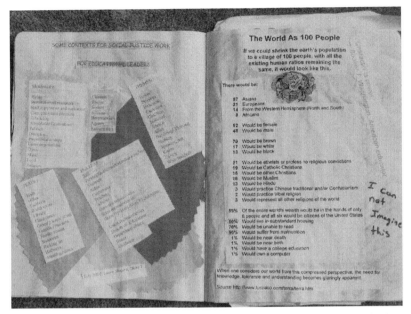

Figure 4.13. Inside Lindsey's journal—contexts for social justice work (Shapiro, 2004).

Valli (1997) codified and defined teacher reflection into types: reflection in/on action, deliberative, personalistic, and critical. Describing personalistic reflection as a developmental process, Valli articulates its focus. It is, he says, "teacher's voice, personal growth, and professional relations [that] are of primary concern" (p. 219). Although many students' reflective processes fell under this rubric, critical reflection expressed through both written and arts processes resulted as well. Lindsey's (2007 class) reflective journal entries, gracing preceding pages and in the pages that follow, are poignantly illustrative of such critical reflection and mythically exemplify her personal reflectivity, as well.

Figure 4.14. Lindsey's journal entries—personal and critical reflection side-by-side, 2007.

During her interview, Phaedra (2006 class) talked about art as an essential tool for reflection and its ability to connect her to her emotions, allowing her to feel and to learn in a deeper way. Phaedra helped answer the question, "What role does reflection through the arts play in the classroom culture?"

It was the arts that really set it apart from the other courses. I hold onto the course feeling-wise. I can feel the course and how I felt in the course in such a deeper way. It was the emotional piece of really personally reflecting on it (learning) that was really, really intense. (P.G., interview, 8-30-07, p. 2)

Feeling and emotion, as a sub-textual theme and motivator for social justice work runs, like a silver thread, throughout the data. The arts can generate, synthesize, and transform emotion. In addition, Shapiro's (2006) research indicates that art acts as an accelerant for the "intensity and pace of participants' emotional connection with and intellectual understanding of social justice issues . . . " (p. 246). I am certain that the reader has already felt and will continue to feel the undertow and effects of emotion as it plays out in the data on each page of this chapter. I will continue to highlight this subtheme as it emerges from the data and interweave it throughout the paper in the context of the topic under discussion. Right now, I will continue the discussion on the theme of reflection in some of its other manifestations.

Mask-making as Reflection Tool

Although students were free to explore any of the class exercises in whatever medium suited them at the time, I strongly suggested that students use mask-making to reflect on and explore issues of social justice that were identified during and after viewing the documentary film, The Letter, to which I alluded earlier. By inviting my students to be mindful of the polarities being played out in the documentary, my aim was to help them organize, process, and reflect on what was going on in the situation depicted in the documentary, a situation wrought with discrimination and racial hatred, as well as courage and voice. The following is a composite list of student-generated polarities.

Figure 4.15. Student dramatization "The Faces of Discrimination," 2006.

Trust	Fear
Voice	Silenced
Native	Outsider
Hate	Acceptance
Haves	Have Nots
Stereotypes	Real People
Courage	Cowardice
Dialogue	Stonewall
Blame	Responsibility
Ignorance	Acceptance
Violence	Non-Violence
Power Over	Power With
Competitive	Cooperative
Male Power	Female Power
Collaborative	Polarizing
Leader as Active	Leader as Passive (Aggressive)
Need	Greed
Divided	United
Poverty	Privilege
Muslim	Christian
Citizen	Foreigner
Listening	Hearing
Hatred	Forgiveness
Acceptance	Rejection
Privilege	Disadvantage
Deserving	Undeserving
Equality	Discrimination
Resources	Lack of Resources
Coming Together	Tearing Apart
Abundance Thinking	Deficit Thinking
Cultural Heritage	Colonizing Culture

Figure 4.16. Student-generated composite list of polarities (flip chart notes, 2006-2008).

I urged my students to use mask-making as a form of reflection and, beginning with a student-generated list of polarities that were evoked during and after viewing the film as a spring board for reflection and exploration ground for these polarities. Using the outside of the mask *and* the inside of the mask gave students a double canvas on which they were able to illustrate the two poles of the issues they identified.

In keeping with the use of the arts to identify, explore, and address social justice issues as an alternative means of teaching social justice education, the poet, William Blake, with his emphasis on perception, poetry, and spirit as ways of exploring and understanding reality was my muse for the mask-making (for reflection) exercise I facilitated.

> Cruelty has a Human Heart
>
> And Jealousy a Human Face:
>
> Terror, the Human Form Divine
>
> And Secrecy, the Human Dress.
>
> The Human Dress is Forged Iron,
>
> The Human Form, a fiery Forge;
>
> The Human Face, a Furnace seal'd,
>
> The Human Heart, its hungry Gorge.(William Blake, in Mizanoglu, 1998, p. 51)

Figure 4.17. Student reflection through mask-making.

Tia's (2007 class) mask and artist's statement illustrates how deep exploration, reflection, and understanding are made possible through the creative process. Mask-making provided Tia with a reflective tool and another lens through which to view polarities.

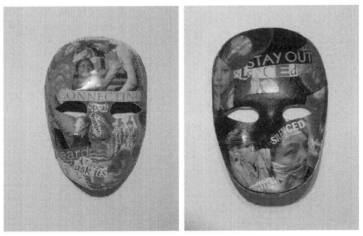

Figure 4.18. Student mask—being heard and being silenced, 2007.

Tia's (2007 class) artist's statement describes "being heard" and "being silenced," the polarities upon which she reflected and set out to represent:

> This mask represents the polarities of *being heard* and *being silenced*. On the outside I chose to represent *being heard*. A person is heard when they are

looked at and *seen*. When a person is *silenced* they are ignored and *not seen*. I chose to represent that polarity on the inside of my mask. Being a teacher, I feel it is very important for all students to be heard and to feel valuable and significant while they are learning. I hope that as I grow as a teacher I will always remember to listen and try to ensure that all my students have a voice. (T.A., artist's statement, 2007)

In her mask, Beatrice (2007 class) reflects on oppression. The following excerpt from her journal provides a window through which we can observe her reflective process:

One cannot simply look at a person and tell if they have been socially oppressed or (if they have) caused social oppression. In creating my mask I made that uncertainty a reality. I painted the face of my mask in all black to represent the darkness of social oppression and how it brings society down. I then used yellow paint to create lightning to illustrate how social oppression stings and causes chaos in society. The inside of my mask was the opposite of oppression, which in my mind, were rainbows of color. All these colors united are a force of power bigger than oppression, overcoming it. (B.C., student journal, 2007, p. 5)

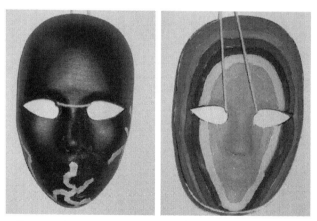

Figure 4.19. Face of oppression and rainbow of color, 2007.

Artist's Statement

In the face of oppression I will fight,

In the face of oppression I will struggle,

In the face of oppression I will fear the unknown,

In the face of oppression I will encounter obstacles,

In the face of oppression I will smile,

In the face of oppression I will allow all of my strength and beauty to be seen,

This revealing of myself will be too powerful for oppression to survive,

Oppression will be defeated and all that will be left is my rainbow of pride.

(B.C., artist's statement, 2007)

In Beatrice's vision, beauty and self-revelation overcome oppression. The urge toward action for change is apparent in both Tia's and Beatrice's statements.

Ellen (2006 class) likens her mask-making to a nonverbal tipping point (Gladwell, 2002) where everything in the course came together for her:

When I constructed my mask, I was already getting in touch with my inner voice but I didn't know it until I started working on the mask. I had lots to say without using one word. From there I just grew-from inside out. When I read the (assigned) literature after this point, everything had a new meaning, a new interpretation. (E.F., student journal entry, 2006)

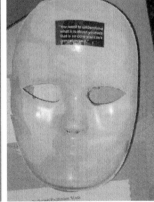

Figure 4.20. Mask—inclusion and exclusion, 2007.

For my students, reflection through mask-making yielded self-revelation, self-acceptance, finding and allowing voice with passionate feeling, reflection on justice issues, and an impulse to action for change. Additionally, mask-making, created a complex pathos for reflection on larger issues of social justice, opening the doors to sustained empathic *dialogue*, the next theme that I will discuss.

Emotion and Action

Emotion and action are recurring subthemes, surfacing again and again as students describe their experiences and the unique quality of the classroom culture. Dissanayake (1992, 2000), reminds us of the ancient role the arts played in harnessing and utilizing the emotion generated by and through the arts for making sense and acting on the world—just as art can do today at the service of social justice education. She says

> It seems likely that the early humans who wished to "do something" in response to problems and fears they faced would have found, as we and our children do today, emotional satisfaction and calm in the "controlled" behavior of shaping time and space, of putting these into comprehensible forms. (1992, p. 83)

Carrie (2007 class), in her self-learning and evaluation paper, captures an essential function of the arts to bring our emotional content to the surface and tap our *feeling* selves. She sums up the power of the arts as a reflective tool that allows us to release emotion, making feelings intelligible, and finding our voice in relation to the issues of social justice that are being explored. "My artwork led the way," she wrote, "and then I found the words to express my feelings" (C.C., self-learning and evaluation paper, 7-07, p. 4). Like Ellen (2006 class), art-making allowed Carrie a deeper and wider understanding through nonverbal means and her art led the way. Art-making allowed students to put their feelings into comprehensible form and give form to unspoken and sometimes incomprehensible feelings.

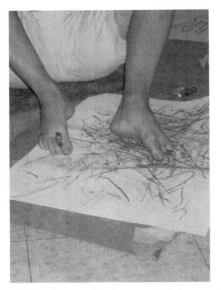

Figure 4.21. Student uses her feet to scribble her emotions, 2007.

Emotion and action were recurring themes in students' comments about the culture of the course. The ability of arts to generate, process, and to be applied as a balm for the emotion generated appears to strengthen the rationale for their use and efficacy in social justice education. Beatrice (2007 class) speaks explicitly about how emotion, resulting from the autobiographical art processes, connects to commitment to social justice action in the world:

> Creating this poem (I Am From) helped me work through a lot of anger, confusion, love, frustration, happiness, and sadness I have held in my heart and has penetrated my soul. Writing those words did not come easy because it make all those emotions even more real and thus forced me to confront them. Thinking about those emotions was even more of a challenge because I could not block them out any longer, I had to allow them to rise to the surface of my heart and allow them to be seen. After I was completely done with my poem, I felt such a satisfaction and pride in myself for allowing myself to put a stop to the roadblock I have put on my heart and soul. Reading it over now I see even more how social oppressions such as poverty, abuse, drugs, discrimination, sexism, religion, and violence have affected my life. I realized how much of a

desire I have to work against these oppressions and all forms of oppression. (B.C., self-learning and evaluation paper, 8-1-07, pp. 3-4)

Similarly, reading Maya's (2006 class) description of her experience during the student retrospective show provides a window through which to actually see her emotion (generated by the artwork), and how it moved her to a deep understanding and learning about leadership.

> I remember walking over to Caren's work first, I started reading her educational autobiography and then I read her "I Am From" (poem). Mid-way through the piece, tears started to flow. . . . These weren't tears of empathy, or sadness . . . I was crying because Caren and I came from two totally different life experiences, I mean here she was, this rural girl from open fields, crocheting, and family dinners. I was from the streets of Brooklyn where "stick and can" was the best game around, and crack was available at every corner. All I kept saying to myself while reading her piece was, "How can we ever relate? How could I ever know what she feels? How can she ever know what I feel?" Then I realized that's why we're here, to learn these things. If we don't know how to feel, we don't know how to be leaders. (M.B., self-evaluation paper, 7-28-07, p. 2)

As I read Alan's (2008 class) final paper, I was struck by the power of his metaphors as he described the enmeshment of art and emotion. I am intrigued with the way Alan described his learning process as "lessons that found him" (A.B., final paper, 2008, p. 3).

> Art is emotion. Emotions are often labeled as abstract. They exist within us but cannot survive outside of us. How naïve. Art is emotion and exists because of emotion. . . . Art is the microphone that gives voice to these emotions. (A.B., final paper, 2008, p. 3)

For me, Alan's realization that art is the microphone that gives voice to emotion sums up not only a key theme that emerged from the data, but also the reason the arts pack such a powerful punch as a reflection, inquiry, and dialogue tool for social justice teacher education. In the next section, I will continue the exploration of emotion and examine one emotion in particular—fear. Fear appears to be amplified through the arts and has the potential to inhibit learning if not anticipated, voiced, understood, and addressed.

Fear of the Arts

As we have seen, a spectrum of emotions can be stirred up through creating and viewing works of art. Fear of art has been evident throughout my 15-year career of teaching the expressive arts, and fear of the arts consistently emerged as a very strong subtheme in the data I collected over the last three years. In 2007, I incorporated a visit to the campus museum into the course, hoping it would help students overcome their reticence to the arts. I had three specific objectives in mind when I designed the museum visit:

1. To assist students in overcoming their fear of art by breaking down the walls, which they and others have built over the course of their lives that separate them from art and the art-making process. Over the last 15 years of teaching the expressive arts, I have heard students repeatedly say things like, "I am not an artist. I can't make art. I am afraid of art. I don't understand art."

2. To help students develop a way of seeing, what Greene (1995) calls *deep noticing,* that would help them make connections between the work of art, their own lives, the larger world, and ultimately, issues of justice and fairness.

3. To use the works of art, exhibited at the museum, to inspire students in their own art-making processes to help them release their imaginations (Greene, 1995), expand their notions of what art is and help them experience the power of the arts as vital meaning-making and communication tools for leadership and change.

To accomplish these goals, I utilized the Lincoln Center Institute's capacities for aesthetic education as a guiding framework (see Appendix D for the document "Teaching and Learning at the Lincoln Center Institute") and crafted several essential questions to help guide my students and encourage them to identify with a work of art by relating to it personally as an autobiography (see Appendix E for the document "Guidelines for the Dorskey Museum of Art Session"). The capacities for aesthetic education were inspired by Maxine Greene, the Institute's philosopher in residence for many years. I felt that using the capacities as a framework might help my students become familiar with the arts in a personal, non-threatening way. After all, I was not asking them to make art, but simply to interact with it. Ultimately, I hoped the experience would build the foundation for the use of the arts for social justice. The results were mixed, but did provide an opportunity for a closer examination of fear.

The following excerpt from Jessica's (2007 class) journal gives a representative flavor of what many of my students were feeling that night.

I have to admit, when I was first told that we were leaving the safety and comfort of an Old Main classroom to go to an art gallery, I was not excited. I never really understood art, or the art process, and it was hot out; I definitely did not want to walk across campus. When I arrived at the show, I felt that feeling that I usually feel around art. Overwhelmed and anxious, this is the exact opposite of what art is supposed to make you feel like. I tried to keep an open mind and listened to the directions given. (J. B., student journal—reaction to art show, 7-07, p. 1)

Reading Jessica's journal was like reading many student journals in the past. Certainly not all, but many students' first response to art is anxiety, trepidation, tension, or fear. As a humanistic educator, I was confused, conflicted, and concerned by my student's fear and wondered how many other students might be feeling the same way, but not revealing their feelings. I strongly believe that students need a non-threatening, safe environment in order to learn. With so many of my students expressing discomfort, I had to question my use of the arts and there were times I thought, "Perhaps the arts are *not* 'for everyone.'"

The following passage from my teaching journal will give the reader a glimpse of the questions that I wrangled with:

I want to understand why Jessica and so many of her peers fear art, fear something that Dissanayake wants us to understand (reclaim?) as a primal human behavior, necessary for survival; one that provides emotionally soothing and satisfying experiences. Perhaps art has been so marginalized in daily life (by whom? deliberately? to what purpose?) that it has come to belong to and to represent only an elite few who understand it, value it (or some of it), commoditize, and consume it. By losing our connection (or having it taken from us?) to the behavior of "making special" (Dissanayake, 1992), individually and in community, allowing emotion to move us to action, and using the creative process to help us re-consider and re-create our world, we have become separated from a vital source of our power, birthright, and humanity. (Barbera, 2007b, p. 10)

I was clearly struggling to understand how we had drifted so far from our birthright. If Dissanayake (1992) is correct, when she posits that art-making was a selectively developed evolutionary behavior, as necessary for survival as food, clothing, and shelter, why did students exhibit so much iitial fear of art? Had they lost the biologic wisdom that, according to Dissanayake, is basic to their and our survival? Dissanayake helps to grasp the importance and the function of art as a necessary human behavior.

> As a human ethologist, I consider myself a materialist in that I wish to trace human behavior to its deepest material or physical roots, and to establish that, like human anatomy and physiology, it [art] is ultimately in the service of a our biological adaptation and survival. Yet I find the standard materialist position with regard to art to be inadequate, for it unthinkingly accepts the modern belief that art is extraneous. My position, lone as it might be, is that making important activities special has been basic and fundamental to human evolution and existence, and that while making special is not strictly speaking in all cases art, it is true that art is *always* an instance of making special. (p. 92)

By placing the contemporary view of the arts in its proper historical and cross-cultural context, Dissanayake (1992) assisted me in putting Jessica's fear in perspective.

> We must not forget that although "Art" as a concept seems to have been born of and continues to be sustained by a commercial society, is therefore only roughly two centuries old, and hence is relative, even discardable, *the arts* have always been with us. And so have ideas of beauty, sublimity, and transcendence, along with the verities of the human condition: love, death, memory, suffering, power, fear, loss, desire, hope, and so forth. These have been the subject matter of and occasion for the arts throughout human history. Thus, when contemporary theory accepts that art is contingent and dependent on "a particular social context," the mistake should not be made of assuming that the abiding human concerns and the arts that have immemorially been their accompaniment and embodiment are themselves contingent and dependent. (p. 41)

Figure 4.22. Students at the Dorsky Museum, July 2007.

Many of my students had a similar mind set about art as Jessica did initially, believing that art is for a select group of people, out of their realm, or something they do not or cannot understand. They did not see art as something that belonged to *them*, as an integral part of *their* biological make up, *their* birthright, or as ultimately useful or necessary to *them*. Dissanayake (1992) says that most of us understand art only through a modern lens "within a narrow, modern, Western paradigm of art as something rare and elite" (p. 96).

Kelly (2006 class) speaks from this paradigm for many students in the following excerpt from her self-learning and evaluation paper and, like many students, given time, gradually emerged from her self-imposed exile from the arts to a new relationship with them, as well as with herself:

> I came to this course with some trepidation. I have no talent for the arts. I can't sing, draw, paint, dance, or anything else that requires innate talent. . . . I decided that I would stick it out and see what happened next. And what happened next was a great experience. (K.K., self-learning and evaluation paper, 7-30-06, p. 1)

Ellen (2006 class) expressed her reticence and subsequent opening to the arts in this way:

> This course was a true "journey" for me. Let me start right from the beginning. It is 7:30 p.m. on July 5, 2006 and I am thinking, "What the hell am I doing

here"? . . . WHY am I here? I don't belong here. I made a big mistake—let me out. But I did return for the next class after my friend reminded me that we will be three credits closer to our goal (when the course is over). OK, let's just stick it out I thought. What changed my mind was the expressive arts activity. (E.F., reflection paper, 2006, p. 1)

Crysta (2008 class) grapples with fear during an improvisational drama exercise and, by doing so, gives insight into how she overcame her fear. Interestingly, she relates her fear of art to her fear of leadership:

Fear held me back from expression and could hold me back from leadership. Fear of judgment, shame, and change. The experience was very new to me and scary at first. . . . I felt out of my comfort zone. This experience showed me I need to identify what my fears are before I can work through them and I can use artistic expressions to work through them. (C.V., 8-08-08, p. 4)

Amazingly, the very thing she feared—art—emerged as her antidote for fear. Bayles and Orland (1993), in their groundbreaking work, *Art and Fear: Observations on the Perils and Rewards of Art-Making*, concur with Crysta. When difficulties arise around making art, they advise to "follow the leads that arise from contact with the work itself, and your technical, emotional and intellectual pathway becomes clear" (p. 113). Listen to the transformation of Jessica's feelings by the end of her first journal entry:

Overall, despite my initial objections, I found this experience to be a fantastic gateway to this class. I learned that I was going to have to let go of my left-brain for awhile. I am still not comfortable with the whole idea, but I am definitely making progress. (J.B., student journal—reaction to art show, 7-07, p. 3)

Hilly (2007 class) compares her museum visit on the first day of class to the retrospective show at the end of the course, in bookend fashion. Her evolutionary process is astounding, as she moves from feeling totally out of her element at the Dorskey Museum to her new self-identification as an artist in just four weeks:

Like it's a culture within a culture, just to move from one environment to the other. It's like where was I? I was back in another art [gallery]. When I got over there I remembered the first day. It's funny, the first day and the last day. I had a fear and everything has been worked out throughout the process and at the end of the process here I am in another museum again. That was really powerful I can tell you! I thought, "Oh, I am a part of this. I am a part of this process" and I just see that unfold. And so I appreciated everything that the other [Dorskey Museum] artists did but I think I appreciated this [Retrospective Show] more because I was one of the artists. (H.B., interview, 8-28-07, p. 9)

Figure 4.23. Student lends a work of art—"Her" Life, Samuel Dorsky Museum, 2006.

Gladys' (2007 class) journey through her fear of the arts echoes Jessica's journey. Both used the arts to assist them in working through their fear. Going from *fear* of art to *embracing* art, Gladys said, as the course was coming to a close

I was always anxious about artwork . . . but now I learned to appreciate art more just by using the different modalities. I can just start something and just let it flow. I think that's one of the main things I take away, is not to be afraid. I don't have to fear anymore. I just let it flow and its okay. (G.S., transcription audio recording, 2007, p. 1)

98

Figure 4.24. Dramatization—students embodying fear of judgment and shame, 2008.

Figure 4.25. Dramatization—students embodying resolution, hope, and vision, 2008.

As I look through my transcribed flip-chart notes, which capture students' oral feedback after participating in improvisational dramatizations exploring fear and their subsequent discussion in dialogue groups, many other voices and new insights are added to the mix—coaxing fear into the light of understanding. Following are some of the comments students made about their fear of art:

Fear that art will be judged and criticized

Art exposes and lays bare

Art exposes and leaves venerable

Art never lies always tells the truth-exposes

Art is for the chosen few

Art is intense

Art is not valued in the culture

Art is not taken seriously

Art is the first to be cut (from school budgets)

Fear of non-structured nature of art

Fear of emotion (transcribed flip chart notes, 7-26-08)

The flip chart notes demonstrate that the dialogue group explored not only the negative (represented by fear), but also the positive dimensions of how the arts function. I will list these positive dimensions as well, to balance my reporting of their thoughts on the arts:

Art helps find self

Art creates compassion and empathy for others

Art puts you in the present moment/zone/flow

Arts as a way to communicate

Art as universal language/cultural bridge

We can all make art

Art is social justice work

Social justice work as transformative/help others use same process

Art helps to confront difficult issues

Art is key to the soul

Art never lies, it always tells the truth/exposes. (transcribed flip chart notes, 7-26-08)

For me, these data indicate how many students experienced an initial caution/fear of the arts followed by, and sometimes in tandem with, a sophisticated understanding and appreciation of the power of the arts to *identify* ("art never lies"), *explore* ("confront difficult issues"), and *address* ("art creates compassion and empathy for others") social justice issues. Interestingly, art as exposing self/truth was seen as something to fear on a personal level, but, paradoxically, as an aspect of art's strength (on a collective level) for social justice work.

Worthy of note are the two statements, "Art is social justice work," and "Social justice work for transformation and to help others use the same process." At my dissertation proposal hearing, one of my committee members, Dr. Laurien Alexandre, used the same words in her feedback to me as we were discussing the emerging theme of fear. When I came upon the same sentiment in the transcribed notes, I was surprised, at first, to read the exact words. But, as I reflected, it began to make total sense. The logic was flawless—social justice is about fairness, equity, and distribution of power.

Art, as a tool for examining and enriching one's life and inquiring about these issues, is in itself a powerful tool to which everyone is entitled.

The second statement, "Social justice work for transformation and to help others use the same process," indicates to me that, when students experience the transformative power of the arts, they want to help others experience the same and demonstrates how the arts motivate action for change. For me, this brings to mind Scarry's (1999) hypothesis about beauty. Beauty begs to be replicated and that is why it is so closely tied to justice.

Rogers (1993), a pioneer in the field of expressive arts, has witnessed countless examples of the dynamic of fear associated with an introduction or re-introduction to the arts. She articulates the dimensions of fear as "fear of criticism, fear of failure, fear of being misunderstood, fear of the unknown," which she says "may hold us back from using our innate creativity" (p. 23). For Rogers, creating a safe environment is critical in facilitating creativity and addressing the resultant fear that can accompany forays into the arts, and into the self. "It takes a skilled facilitator," she says, "for that kind of caring community to evolve" (pp. 24-25). The skills to which she refers are the psychological safety and freedom espoused by her father, Carl Rogers, and include, empathy, congruence, and unconditional positive regard. I believe the culture of the "'"Expressive Arts, Leadership, and Change" class meets this definition, judging by the outcome for the students.

As we have seen, Hilly (2007 class), Jessica (2007 class), Kelly (2006 class), Ellen (2006 class), and Gladys (2007 class) proved that it is possible for students to move beyond their fear of art and reclaim art as a *way of being* (Rogers, 1980) and as a way of imagining that allows students to envision the world in a new way. I believe providing this opportunity is an essential component in co-creating an arts-based culture for the exploration of social justice in teacher education.

Dialogue

At this point in my inquiry, I am, again, keenly aware that the themes of identity, reflection, dialogue, and community are totally interconnected and, as this report progresses, it becomes more and more of a challenge to separate them into categories under discreet headings. However, in the service of continuity of form, I will continue to attempt to do so.

Figure 4.26. Students in dialogue groups, 2007.

As I look back on my interview with Hilly (2007 class) at her home a month after the class has ended, her experience typifies our culture's elitist paradigm of art, her struggle to overcome that mindset, her shift to feeling more trusting of the arts as a process tool, and the power of *dialogue* to help her process her experience and shift her thinking:

> So it was really, really hard for me going there. I was really taken out of my comfort zone with that one. And I really put up a good front. I had to put up a good front but it was at the end . . . a little bit, I started to feel a little bit free once I started talking. It was like whatever was inside was coming out. So when you had the gathering and we sat around I was like "Wow! This is amazing!" (H.B., interview, 8-28-07, p. 4)

Figure 4.27. Students dialogue with Lucy Barbera, Dorsky Museum of Art, 2007.

The "gathering" to which Hilly refers is the dialogue group processing I facilitated, which allowed students to dialogue about their experience at the Dorskey Museum, after doing so in pairs, with the entire class. I could almost hear a collective sigh of relief when students begin to share their journey and began to realize that others felt the same anxiety, curiosity, empathy, or pleasure that they were feeling.

Palmer (1998) identifies what he calls necessary *paradoxes* as he explores the dimensions of pedagogical design and key elements of a responsive learning environment. "The learning space," he says, "should invite the voice of the individual and the voice of the group" (p. 74). As I mentioned earlier, opportunities for dialogue in dyads and triads (the essential units of community), as well as in larger groups, were consciously designed into each exercise to give students the opportunity to communicate and discuss personal and professional reflections, emotions, thinking, and learning that was generated through their art-making, as well as to tackle essential questions about how their experience and learning related to social justice action. The data indicate that dialogue alone, and in tandem with the arts, and the sharing that dialogue allowed helped students reveal aspects of themselves on a very deep level and, incrementally, build a sense of trust as the basis for community.

Figure 4.28. Students dialogue in dyads, 2006.

Hilly (2006 class) describes this phenomenon neatly:

> We started to know each other as the weeks went by, even though we didn't spend months together. I think that we started connecting. People were more open to express themselves, and just reflect and to share. And as we started sharing, I think we started coming together, forming our little bond there. I think it's the sharing part of it. (H.B., interview, 8-28-07, p. 3)

Patton addresses the efficacy of the dialogue process for social justice education. When I asked him if anything about the classroom culture moved him closer to understanding more about himself personally and/or professionally in relation to social justice, this is what he had to say

> The class helped me to realize issues of social justice by providing a place for dialogue, which empowered everyone to make change. The class did not simply talk about social justice; it gave avenues for expression with social justice issues. It provided a medium for exchange of ideas and it empowered the students to take steps towards creating change. (P.B., written response to interview questions, 11-07, p. 1)

104

Figure 4.29. Students use art as a springboard for dialogue, 2007.

Dialogue groups provided a "medium for exchange" to which Patton eloquently refers. Students alternated between individual work, reflection, and dialogue. Obviously, students had differing points of view, but were more readily able to listen and respect each others' perspectives, coming, as they did, from a place of mutual respect, based on recognition of each person's value and worth. The data indicate that the genesis of the development of respect stemmed from the identity work that was shared in dialogue at the outset of the course.

Phaedra (2006 class) describes the development of the culture as an evolutionary process, rooted in reciprocal self-revelation, and the role that art played in facilitating that mutual self-revelation:

> There is definitely an evolution of the classroom culture as the course went on and I think that a big part of that was how the arts fell into the aspects that we often think of as raw. And I think that through making artwork. . .we ended up exposing parts of ourselves to each other...I felt like we really began to know each other through that. . . .The methods that you use to get to social justice were highly effective, so we could see each other and identify with each other, and I think relate to each other in a way just respectfully of that place of being vulnerable together and I think that that made a really big difference. (P.G., interview, 8-30-07, p. 1)

Art-making, tied to dialogue and emotion for Tia (2007 class), was the transforming agent, bringing students together to create an empathic classroom culture based on authenticity. Tia expresses it this way:

> I think it is the honest and understanding nature of my classmates and teacher that helped me to be more honest. I was touched and moved by the openness of others that I felt inspired to be more open with my own inner feelings and was not afraid to be more honest with myself. Through creating expressive pieces of artwork I was able to realize my true inner feeling and was able to release those emotions in a productive and inspiring way. (T.A, written response to interview questions, 10-6-07, p. 2)

For Katie (2006 class) art-making gave an "escape into the world of freedom of expression and emotion" (K.P., written response to interview questions, 10-8-07, p. 2) and *dialogue* was a key component of the classroom culture that moved her closer to understanding more about herself personally in relation to social justice. She wrote:

> The (art) processes, discussion, and the experiences we talked about in class, moved me closer to understanding myself personally in relation to social justice. . . . With discussing topics in small groups, I learned how to work with those who had a different point of view than me, but wanted similar goals. It helped me realize attributes I possess as a leader and I was able to learn from others how to become an even stronger leader for others. (K.P., written response to interview questions, 10-8-07, p. 2)

Figure 4.30. Students in dialogue, 2007.

Don (2007 class) expressed the power of dialogue in creating a positive classroom culture in this way:

> There was a real, deliberate attempt that socialization was a conscious component of the curriculum. You were actively attempting to get us to interact with one another in a substantive way. I mean we didn't have to learn not to take a hit swing at each other and take turns but we were still learning deeply important ways to regard one another. It sort of gave us our humanity back a little bit. (D.C., interview, 9-2-07, p. 7)

Students' professional concerns were also brought to dialogue group forums where students could grapple with justice issues they encountered in their schools on a daily basis and through dialogue attempt to collaboratively create a plan of action to address these issues.

Dialogue was generated around students' life stories, poetry, and visual art in relation to social justice. As Patton (2007 class) reported, students were not merely sharing their thoughts on social justice in dialogue groups—they were sharing their personal experiences around equity and justice as it related to their lives. They were doing this through their creative artwork, poetry, song, dramatic improvisations, life map-making, mask-making, and other multimedia art as well. Students were not simply intellectually inquiring about issues of social justice, but were inquiring experientially through visual and performing art processes (dramatic improvisations, song, music) as a springboard to dialogue about their feelings and discoveries, imagining alternative realities and the action needed to lead them there.

Community

The student retrospective show is where *identity* and *reflection* met in *dialogue* to solidify and celebrate *community*. On the second-to-last day of class, before the students presented their final action plans on the last day of class, I invite them to mount all of their artwork, including painting, drawing, poetry, life maps, mandalas, masks, and their artist statements accompanying their work. The show brought everyone together as a community in a dynamic relationship where individual students recognized their unique journey, while simultaneously honoring the other students in the community, recognizing their journeys as well. The results, as will be revealed in this section, are a dazzling testimony to the power of the arts to knit individuals empathically together in a bonded and cohesive community.

Figure 4.31. Students set up the retrospective show, 2007.

Dissanayake (1990) cautions would be change agents of the need to go beyond their individual explorations in the arts and think and act collectively through them for mutual good:

> Those who would transform the world or solve its problems must choose whether to begin first with the society or the individual. . . . And although art in its present Western sense can indeed affect individuals-by intimating to them "universal meanings" and by enriching, deepening, and ramifying their experience—it is questionable whether, abstracted from social life, it will have

any effect on the evolutionary fitness of the species. Because human beings have evolved to live together committed to one another in social groups, it would seem that individual attempts to find only individual fulfillment perilously ignore the constraints of the human heritage. (pp. 195-196)

Expressive Arts, Leadership, and Change students were involved in both individual transformation, as well as collective transformation. The data indicate that the two processes (individual and collective) for them were not mutually exclusive. The themes that emerged from the students' retrospective show centered on collective *reflection, dialogue,* and *community building.* Year-one students (2006) were invited to participate in year-two students' (2007) retrospective show. Both of these groups of students were invited to year-three's (2008) retrospective show. Four students from the 2006 class chose to come and participate in the 2007 class show; three students from the 2006 class and one student from the 2007 class chose to participate in the 2008 retrospective show—creating a rich cross-fertilization of the culture (generationally) over time.

As a unifying gesture, each of the visiting students were invited to read their "I Am From" poems during the show and after the show meet with the current students in dialogue groups to discuss essential questions brought up by the course. In 2007, the 2006 students seemed to enter into the stream of the current classroom culture as effortlessly as if they had been members of the group from the beginning. Don, a year one student, describes his (original and subsequent) retrospective experiences:

It was a spiritual experience in there. I don't think I am going overboard to say that. I will not soon forget how I felt during that retrospective session that we did. It felt great to revisit that again. It all came back. I felt like I got to know your students more in those couple of hours than many people that I have been with for years. (D.C., interview, 9-1-07, p. 14)

Hilly goes on to cite the culminating retrospective show as representing a core aspect of the classroom culture: "[the] retrospective show was a culture by itself. . . . It wasn't the cherry on top of the ice cream. I was more like in the middle. It was more like the core of everything coming together" (H.B., interview, 8-27-07, p. 9).

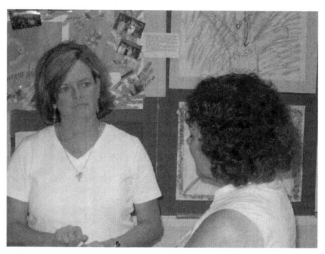

Figure 4.32. Deep listening and dialogue, 2007.

Tia, in her written response to my interview questions, also uses the retrospective show to shed light on the unique culture of the classroom:

> One experience that I felt reflected the classroom culture was our retrospective show. I remember when I tried to read my "I Am From" poem and just couldn't do it, my classmates did not judge me as weak or anything negative. Instead, I received a hug and each person was understanding about how emotional it could be to stand up in front of everyone and read a poem about where I am from and who I am from. I was really touched by my other classmates' courage, strength, and honesty and a week later I read my "I Am From" poem to my sister. I just thought about how supportive and understanding my classmates were and feel blessed to have met each one of these people. (T.A., interview, 10-8-07, p. 3)

The empathy and mutual compassion are palpable as I recollect the incident that Tia is describing. As it so happened, Tia's "I Am From" poem was written with her sister in mind (from whom she was estranged) and, as a result, she was not speaking to the person she wanted most to hear it. Her fellow students did not know this at the time but sensed it and responded compassionately with empathy and congruence.

Figure 4.33. Deep noticing, retrospective show, 2007.

Compassion, Connection, Unity

Throughout the course, dialogue groups had afforded students a home base, or place to process, explore, and question their experiences and the proceedings of the day. After the retrospective show, dialogue groups met, so students could ground their experience and collect their thoughts and emotions through mutual discourse. There were just enough former students present to have one representative in each of the dialogue groups. The essential question I posed for the 2007 dialogue groups was "How do autobiography, the arts, and emotion act to catalyze action for social justice?"

Gratefully, one of my students took legible journal notes of her dialogue group's responses which help to shed light on this group's multifarious thinking about this question, while honoring the dialogue, community, and unity processes they pursued together:

It opens you up to what's real.

You dig deep into yourself find your heart and compassion and then you can share this with others.

It gives you a really loving, open-minded, eye for others.

It helps create equality in your thought. You share this out into the world and it penetrates others.

111

When you give compassion and kindness, it helps others to open up and give it, too.

Sharing "I Am From" poems and hearing others' comments on artwork—It was uplifting to hear others' lives through their poems and their artwork. (M.G., student journal entry, 7-28-07, pp. 42-43)

Clearly, these students felt that *compassion* is catalyzed through the arts for social justice action.

Additionally, as a community building and reinforcing event, the retrospective show of student work represented the "core of everything coming together," as Hilly so eloquently put it, and a place for "deep knowing," to which Don referred. This collaborative effort appears to exemplify the spirit of the community, variously defined by the students as uplifting and generating empathy, compassion, and higher purpose. As I reflect on what the student dialogue groups reported, several themes, germane to this paper, are reiterated. It appears that the genesis of compassion for others was a result of reflection on their own lives and action was incited by the same process.

In my study of the classroom culture in the Expressive Arts, Leadership, and Change course, I was not surprised to discover the importance of community as an essential ingredient of social justice education and of the culture of the classroom, as well. An authentic experience of community has the potential to galvanize students toward action by connecting them emotionally—giving them the needed camaraderie and confidence to work for social justice in the larger human community.

Not surprisingly, the retrospective show, with its formal elements of collective display, honoring, and processing served as a ritual for communal expression and cohesion. It was the ritual function of the arts, Dissanayake (1992) says, that served to bring humans in touch with their emotions and united them with others through them: "More important . . . for understanding the evolutionary origin and purpose of art as a human behavior, as well as its emotional power, is the close connection between *making special* and ritual ceremony" (p. 66).

Gladys (2007 class) relates her experience of community as giving her a sense of "a higher purpose in life." I include her entire quote below because it touches on so many of the themes that have been explored thus far in relation to the arts and community: higher purpose, self-understanding, connection, and compassion. Listen to the exponential effect and direction outward her experience and learning engendered:

I feel I experienced collaborative and co-creative learning and teaching for a higher purpose in life. I feel, while I connected with the community of our class, I now want to connect with the communities of my work place and my classroom where I teach. I feel compassion for others, I feel connected to others, and I feel I am more aware of nature, other cultures, and of my path in life. (G.S., self-learning and evaluation paper, 2007, p. 11)

What accounts for the strong bonding, connection, and feelings of being in touch with a higher purpose? The data seem to imply that the ritual-like enchantment that the arts induce many play a role in creating a heightened sense of community. Dissanayake (1992) says

Although one may be very aware of body or mind, there is a felt loss of ego; one is danced by the dance, played by the music and becomes an instrument for the activity or experience. Hence, the individual experiences a sense of blending, of dissolving the boundaries between the "I" and "other." (p. 70)

Students did not end with their individual exploration of identity, but used that exploration as a starting point to catapult them into the collectivity and camaraderie of community, exemplified beautifully by the retrospective show. According to my students, the classroom culture was emotionally safe and collaboratively created. It was a place where students experienced a real sense of unity and community. Hilly (2007 class) says

I think there was a unity there. I really think there was a great unity with everyone in the class. And I think everyone of us together created that culture. I think everyone created that culture because we had fun, we cried together. It was like we were in a safety zone. (H.B., interview, 8-28-07, p. 1)

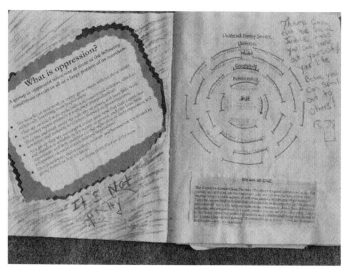

Figure 4.34. Lindsey's journal response to handouts Young (1990), Rogers (1993).

Joy (2007 class), a student working on her school administration post-graduate degree, felt that because students had been able to share of themselves on a deeper level, a rare opportunity for bonding between students resulted. She said, "Classmates shared more about their inner selves, thus allowing us to have a richer, deeper emotional experience and create bonds in the room" (J.D., written response to interview questions, 10-20-07, p. 1). Tia (2007 class) cites community as an essential element of the classroom:

> There was a unique classroom culture in this course. Through our similarities and differences, each person in the class contributed to making our own supportive culture. . . We formed a community that was respectful, understanding, and highly supportive and helpful to all. (T.A., written response to interview questions, 10-8-07, p. 1)

Over and over again, student responses indicate that art-making, combined with dialogue, worked hand-in-hand in building community. Maria says

> Drawing emotions, painting, making mandalas, and then talking about it with the group helped me to see what is behind a person's actions. Working together hands on, expressing ourselves through art also helped us to learn the essential qualities that are necessary when working with other people. (M.G., written response to interview questions, 10-07, p. 1)

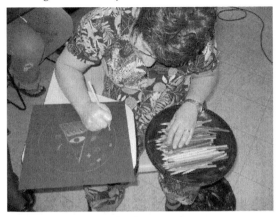

Figure 4.35. Student drawing a mandala, 2007.

Figure 4.36. Student mandala, 2007.

Mandala, an ancient Sanskrit word for circle, has been used throughout time to represent oneness and wholeness (Cunningham, 2002; Fontana, 2005). Over the centuries, circles have been considered a sacred form. Wisdom cultures throughout the world have used mandalas in their rituals to center, align, and bless, by helping community members connect their inner and outer worlds and by bringing people together in unity and community. I utilized mandala-making to help my students integrate their experiences and ground themselves, using their own self-generated healing images. The mandala, or circle, became a dynamic metaphor of community for my students and mandala-making was used on a larger scale, as the course came to a close, to honor our time together and as a bridge back to their lives beyond the course.

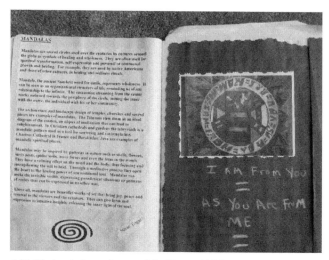

Figure 4.37. Lindsey's journal—mandala (Togut, 2004).

To this end, each student was invited to select a pre-cut, unusually shaped piece of foam core board. I suggested they use any medium of their choice to express what they would bring back to the world from the course.

Figure 4.38. Student creating her Piece of the World, 2007.

When the students finished creating their "Piece of the World," they fit all of their pieces together to form a "World Mandala." Let us watch their collaborative and joyful process.

Figure 4.39. Students assembling World Mandala, 2007.

Figure 4.40. The World Mandala, 2007.

Figure 4.41. Students pass the flame, 2007.

Each student was given a candle and the flame was passed from student to student. Students were then invited to tell about their Piece of the World, what it represented, and what they would take back *from* the course to bring *to* the world. Looking at these photos again reminds me of the deep meaning and attention students gave to this closing ritual and how important it was to help them recollect their experiences and learning, and move forward with clarity. The symbolic meaning inherent in contributing a piece to the world, with each person collaborating to make it whole, was not lost on my students.

Again, Dissanayake (1992) reminds us of the importance of ritual for meaning-making and its central role in culture throughout time, and urges us to reconsider the relevance and necessity of this deep human practice:

> Ritual ceremonies have provided important occasions, during which humans throughout their history have experienced the arts, which themselves were emotionally saturated integral reinforcers of important communal beliefs and

119

truths. In renouncing these . . . we have thus also forfeited the centrality of the arts to life and for making sense of human existence. . . . Without extravagant and extra-ordinary ways to make the significant and serious events of our lives, we relinquish . . . our humanity. (p. 139)

Figure 4.42. Students bring their lights to the world, 2007.

Our final action together as a vibrant learning culture was to, literally and symbolically, light each others' torch and bring them to the world as each student placed their candle on the piece they created.

Figure 4.43. The candlelit World Mandala, 2007.

The following comments were made by students during this closing circle.

What I'll take back is a way to show my students how to collaborate, share feelings, explorations, empower themselves, speak out, build compassion, build empathy, understanding, and caring. (M.G., transcribed audio file, 7-29-07, p. 1)

I'll take reflection, a new sense of self, alliances, awareness, closeness, freedom, focus, and courage. (G.S., transcribed audio file, 7-29-07, p. 1)

I bring confidence in my abilities to express myself through art and also faith in my intuition. (C.D., transcribed audio file, 7-29-07, p. 1)

From this class I take an inner peace in knowing I can make a difference. (L.P., transcribed audio file, 7-29-07, p. 1)

I'll take away from this class the ability to communicate in a new way. I will take back the ability to reflect and the ability to feel again without being seen as weak. (J.B., transcribed audio file, 7-29-07, p. 1)

I will walk away from this class with a new sense of awareness, not just about any kind of "ism" but about the expressive arts and what they can do and how beneficial they can be. (D.B., transcribed audio file, 7-29-07, p. 1)

I'll take from this class an acceptance of myself and also a challenge to become more honest, and courageous, and active in the world. (C.C., transcribed audio file, 7-29-07, p. 1)

From this class, I will take myself. I will take all the energy from this class and produce a better me, a better you, and a better us. Expressive arts will be a part of my curriculum. I will listen, speak, share, express, and definitely paint because now I know I can. I want to paint a new me. (L.O., transcribed audio file, 7-29-07, p. 1)

Summary

Figure 4.44. The unique culture of an arts-based social justice teacher education course, 2006-2008.

My students' closing statements reflect the unique culture of an arts-based social justice teacher education course as they experienced it, and recapitulate the interconnected themes and subthemes of this paper: identity, reflection, dialogue,

122

community, emotion, compassion, fear, and action. These themes demonstrate how the deep value of knowing and appreciating self (identity), taking time to examine justice issues in relation to self and others (reflection), discoursing with others about issues of justice (dialogue), and joining together with others compassionately for change (community) become *palpable* through the arts.

As demonstrated through the research data presented, emotions played in important role in catalyzing personal and professional action for change. Two emotions in particular that were examined were students' fear of art (including why they feared it and how they overcame their fear), and the power of identity, reflection, dialogue, and community to develop compassion for self and others.

The four main themes of identity, reflection, dialogue, and community, emerged naturally from the data and, not surprisingly, align with current research literature in the field (Brown, 2006; Clark, 2005; Clover & Stalker, 2007; Day, C., 2002; Goodson & Numan, 2002; Hatton, 1998; Kenny, 1998; LaBoskey, 2006; Lynn & Smith, 2007; Noel, 2003; Rodgers, 2006; Suominen, 2006) which situates these the themes as essential components of effective social justice education. However, it was *art-making*, the deep sharing of one another's art, and the bonded community that resulted that was the driving process and cultural glue that helped students to synthesize these goals: to know themselves; to know, understand, and value others; and to expand their capacities for working with others in the world for change. The data reveal a resplendent culture, powered by the arts, which created a distinctively *palpable pedagogy* (Barbera, 2006a) for social justice teacher education.

In chapter 5, I will continue to draw conclusions from the research data, discuss the development of my concept of *palpable pedagogy* and its implications for teacher education, and present further suggestions for the continued development and use of pedagogical practices that join mind, body, and heart in social justice teacher education.

Dream

A few days before the first day of teaching Expressive Arts, Leadership, and Change, I had a mystifying dream:

July 8, 2006

Dream: Laura Shapiro and I are at a (conference?). I am changing seats for a better view. I am not focused and I miss most of her lecture. I can hear her but don't comprehend. She's a bit insulted/confused by this. I explain that I don't do very well receptively (through verbal input) and do much better seeing a picture or text.

After the conference, we head to her apartment in the city. One of the trees in the courtyard of Laura's apartment building has lost most of its branches. The branches have become disconnected from the trunk. I point it out to Laura. She is very concerned and seems to be at a loss for what to do. I try to put the branches back into the holes in the tree trunk but they won't stay on their own. I try to hold them in place with a red substance (ketchup?). Only a few of the branches remain on the tree. Those I have put back with the red substance are holding only very tenuously in place.

Figure 5.1. Dream Tree.

I believe that dreams come to assist the dreamer and can provide the dreamer with a teaching, a message from the unconscious, a revelation, or a resolution. So I ask myself, "How is it that this dream is coming to me now, just before the start of my Independent Learning Project with Laura as my mentor for the project? What is the message of the dream, what is it trying to tell me?" I am very happy to be starting this project and to have Laura as my mentor but the dream is "painting another picture." As I begin to unravel the message of the dream, I free associate on the dream's setting, situation, and images.

The dream is set in New York City where Laura has recently moved (in real time). I am a native of New York and feel very much at home there even though I have made my home in the Catskill Mountains for the last 25 years and prefer the natural environment of the country to the city. The setting reminds me of the courtyard of the apartment building where I grew up. It was a lush thick little jungle surrounded by the brick and concrete of a six-story apartment building. Each time I explored it, I discovered something new there. As a child, I often dreamt of being in the courtyard.

I ask myself more questions about the dream. "Why did I choose to use ketchup to secure the tree branches to the tree? Did I feel a need to "catch up" with Laura?" She has done so much work with the arts and social justice. I had assisted her in her dissertation work and it opened my eyes to the endless possibilities and function of the arts for social change. Was I feeling the need to catch up with her because she had been doing this work and I was just beginning to put the pieces of my expressive arts work which had focused on personal healing together with Laura's expressive arts work as an inquiry and collective change tool?

The ketchup reminded me of blood. Reading about the journey of the Gypsies, I learned for the first time about the hundreds of thousands of Gypsies who were killed in the Holocaust. Laura is Jewish; perhaps we share the same blood if we go back far enough. According to Fonseca (1995) a person was considered Jewish if they had a great grandparent who was Jewish. My great grandmother was a Gypsy, so by the formula used by the Nazis to determine who would and would not die, I guess that would make me Gypsy and, had I lived at that time, the target of extermination. Perhaps it is not blood that connects us but the threat, danger, and horror that discrimination posed for our ancestors. Perhaps this is one of the reasons we are both committed to social justice work.

August 30, 2006

Teaching the course is behind me and I reread the tree dream I had before the course started. I want to draw another tree because I realize that this dream tree has no roots. I want to see the roots. It's important for a tree to have roots for stability and nourishment.

Figure 5.2. Roots.

I realize through this process that Laura and I do share the same roots after all, a shared commitment to social justice. We also share the same trunk, our belief in the arts as a meaning-making tool to assist in the critical work of social change.

Figure 5.3. Branches.

It's when I look at the branches, however, that the dream's riddle is solved. Although we share the same roots and trunk, when it comes to the branches we may at times go our separate ways. Perhaps the reason I couldn't put the branches back on Laura's tree is because I need to "branch out" on my own! I know our branches will intertwine as they did in the past and are for the Independent Learning. It was through the creative process of drawing the dream tree again, that I was able to make sense of the dream.

Autobiography: Unfolding Into the Present, Emboldened Into the Future

Looking back, recapturing their stories, teachers can recover their own standpoints on the social world . . . Making an effort to interpret the texts of their life stories, listening to others' stories in whatever "web of relationships" they find themselves, they may be able to multiply the perspectives through which they look upon the realities of teaching; they may be able to choose themselves anew in the light of an expanded interest, an enriched sense of reality. (Greene, 1979, p. 33)

Figure 5.4. Mom, Laura, and Me; Dad and half of our Tribe.

It is day one of Expressive Arts, Leadership, and Change. I am recounting to my students a conversation I had with my advisor, Carolyn Kenny. She was talking about what it was like for her to be entering her sixtieth year. Gesturing with her hands, she said, "The road opens up before me and it opens behind me."

I use this recounting as an introduction to an autobiographical exercise called "I Am From." (Christensen, 2000) I decide to read my "I Am From" to my students to give them a sense of the possibilities that this particular poetic structure offers. I debated with myself about whether or not to read my poem because I did not want students to interpret my poem as the "right" way to do it and for it become a limiting factor.

The other reason I hesitated to read my "I Am From" poem is because it is intensely personal and self-revealing. I had to ask myself, "How much of myself am I willing to share with my students"? After all I could simply read one of the samples Linda Christensen uses in her article describing the process. Ultimately, I read the poem and passed it around after reading it so students can see the picture of my Gypsy Great Grandmother, Eugina Martinelli, of whom I am so proud.

Figure 5.5. Eugina Martinelli.

I Am From

I am from Italian blood.

I am from Sicilian blood.

I am from Gypsy blood.

I am from Grandmothers and Great Grandmothers.

I am from Lara, Eugina, Magdalena, Angelina, and Margarita.

I am from Taconda, Martinelli, Arpino, Ruggerio, and Donata.

I am from Grandfathers and Great Grandfathers.

I am from Luigi, Nicolasanta, Baldessare, and Colegero.

I am from Cisternino.

I am from Barbera.

I am from Brooklyn

Where I was called "Barbarian",

Gypsy, and Black.

I am from a family of ten.

I am from not enough food.

I am from using a hair dryer to keep warm.

I am from no shelter.

I am from being dispossessed.

I am from a father who worked hard but could not find us a place to live.

I am from no one wanting that many kids running around their rental apartments.

I am from "You have too many children."

I am from living in a van.

I am from washing in a wading pool in the city park.

I am from "homelessness" before it was on the evening news.

I am from a mother who had no money for food but fed my artistic spirit with love.

I am from always being different.

I am from telling my mother "I want to be like everyone else."

I am from her response: "Oh no, you don't!"

I am from working on behalf of children who suffer silently.

I am from exposing their subtle and blatant oppressions.

I am from advocating for parents who have not learned how to advocate for themselves.

I am from dedicating my life to helping others.

I am from art for dialogue and healing.

I am from leading from the fringes.

I am from leading from my center.

I am from leading for social justice for all.

Lucy Barbera   July 3, 2006

In January, 2006, at the Seattle residency, Carolyn had asked me what I was thinking about for exploration in my dissertation. I said I wanted to study a "wisdom culture" and find out how change was negotiated in that culture. My suspicion was that creativity had something to do with how "wisdom cultures" created change. When I got home, I wrote to a friend in Tasmania and told him my idea. He wrote back inviting me to come to Tasmania. He is a researcher and has written extensively on the Aboriginal cultures of Australia. He described islands unaffected by the modern world and his connections to the island chiefs and assured me access to this "wisdom culture."

After thinking this over for several months, it occurred to me that the culture of my parents and their parents and their parent's parents was as valid as any "wisdom culture" I could find today. It was this realization that brought me to the study of the Gypsy (or Romany) culture. Through the following autumn and winter, I immersed myself in the study of the history of the Gypsy or Romani people. Fonseaca's (1995) *Bury Me Standing*, was my bible during this period. I scrawled in the margins of every page as memory after memory of my childhood emerged. As I read about the Gypsies and their journey, my life's journey began to make sense in a way it had never done before.

The landscape I had painted so many months before I knew of the horror of the Gypsy's lives during the Holocaust became the setting for my Great Grandmother's picture and the basis of my "I Am From" poem. Of course the other realization I had as I researched the Gypsy culture was that arguably they made up the largest population of "homeless" people in the world. During my very early childhood, my family was homeless. As all of these revelations were unfolding, I was just finishing up a month's long Organizational Change Project facilitating expressive arts training for homeless shelter staff in my community.

Figure 5.6. Autobiographical college.

My journey has taken me from wanting to "find" a "wisdom culture" to study how they initiate and navigate change, identify the principles of dealing with change, and apply these principals, as a school leader, in helping the faculty create change at my school. My intuition was that the creativity, ritual, and spirit would have to play an important role in this process. What I discovered through this study is that the "self" is a wisdom culture" or put another way I discovered "(my)self as wisdom culture" and as such, self as an instrument of change in the world. Most certainly, the arts have something to do with accessing the "wisdom of the self", by bringing us directly in touch with ourselves on our deepest level and connecting us to each other on that level. It is this level that is the source of our "wisdom spring", like the roots of the dream tree this source connects us to others via what I think of as a "universal wisdom spring."

Figure 5.7. Bury Me Standing (Fonseca, 1995).

Figure 5.8. Angelina, an aristocrat, eloped with the Gypsy's son, Luigi.

(They came to America, first Luigi, followed by Angelina with my Mother, Giacoma, and uncle, Lauro, in tow.)

All migrants move in pursuit of a better life; furthermore, those who uproot themselves are often the most enterprising members of their society. (Fonseca, 1995, p. 228)

One of the most enlightening moments of the course came during the Retrospective, when after reading her "I Am From" poem, one of my students said, "I would never have had the courage to write this poem, if I had not experienced the honesty of your poem, Lucy. I probably would have written something very surface, true, but shallow. Your poem gave me the courage to write mine."

During my training with her, Natalie Rogers would often say that self-revelation engenders reciprocal self-revelation and that the extent to which we self-reveal is the extent that we build trust and I would add: community. I think that for my students the first great revelation came when they were able (through the art process) to reveal themselves to themselves. The second revelation came in revealing deep aspects of themselves to another. The third revelation came in revealing themselves "in community," creating their own "wisdom culture" of educators committed to social justice.

I'll close this journal with my Touchstone's (DeCantias, 1996) words

Figure 5.9. Creating Touchstone.

Figure 5.10. My Touchstone speaks.

I am rising up out of the darkness.

I am coming into the light.

I am being released from suffering.

I am being released from oppression.

My bonds are being broken.

My chains are being broken.

I hear the bell of liberation.

I am growing the wings of a bird.

"Touchstone"

Lucy Barbera

January 14, 2007

134

Originally, this autoethnographic journal was conceived of as a way for me to chart my process as a college professor teaching social justice education through the arts. As I pick up the chronicling process this year, I will continue to document my experience in teaching Expressive Arts, Leadership, and Change. My current Independent Learning process centers on the examination of the "culture" of arts-based social justice teacher education. For this autoethnographic journal, I try to have *my* processes mirror those of my students, first, as they explore their identity through autobiographical exercises. Second, the self-reflection I encourage in my students, I employ in this document. And third, this autoethnographic journal allows me to align emotionally and learn along with my students, and is a springboard for dialogue with them and others about my life, my journey, my commitment to social justice and social justice teacher education, my art-making process, and arts-informed inquiry methods. Welcome to my world.

"If my life's story is so small and insignificant . . . it will first exist for me when I can tell it to you and you will listen. . . . "

(Rilke, letter to Lou Andreas-Salome, 2003)

Figure 5.11. Landscape of the Soul.

Figure 5.12. Self-portrait painted on 7-14-07.

I chose self-portrait as a medium to further explore my identity, picking up the thread I started last year. (Barbera, autoethnographic journal, 2006a). I consider self-portrait painting a rare treat and throughout my life have used self-portrait painting as a mirroring process, an inquiry into self in time, a glimpse into my interior world through my painted image. Natalie Rogers (1993) encourages us to employ the "Creative Connection" approach when using the expressive arts. By "creative connection" she means allowing one creative process to flow from another, thus allowing me to go deeper into the message of the feeling and images as the emotion engendered is explored and widened through a recursive exploration in multiple media. To this end, shortly after painting my self-portrait, I began writing as a "creative connection."

136

Free Write 7-21-07

I have had a whole week to gaze at you as you gaze out from the canvas. What strikes me most are your eyes. They are so wide, looking out at me, in surprise and amazement. I look back at you the same way. You look as if you have just come down from the mountains that are now behind you and through a grassy meadow at your back. I can see the shadow of a path behind you. Does that path represent your past? Have you come that way before? Or is it the way you are heading—your future? Where are you heading, toward home or away from home? Where is your home?

You are my aboriginal self. Not just your vision but all of your senses are totally open and receptive, you are taking in information about the landscape ahead, smelling the air, looking for signs ahead of you. Looking for guidance? Listening paused, expectant, you are from another time, my sister. You are from a time long past, witnessing the present, seriously, calmly, intently, and reflectively.

You are surrounded by trees, and above you reigns a turquoise sky. You are in harmony with the landscape you occupy. Your skin is dark. Is it multi-cultural or smeared in red ochre, red of the earth? You are from everywhere; you have come from everywhere, and are going everywhere. You see everything, past, present, and future.

What you have lived and seen is reflected in your face, your expression. As I look into your eyes, I hear your voice; you speak to me in another way. This is what you say:

I am Lucy.
I am you and you are me.
I am from ancient times.
I am from searching.
I am from seeking
I am from listening.
I am from understanding.
I am from many races and cultures.
I am from a world that is full of light and dark, pain and joy, peace and conflict, oppression and liberation, confusion and logic, intuition and reason, polarities and paradox. I am from motherhood, partnership, friendship, leadership.

I am from the mountains, meadow, shadow, light.

I am from the path. I am from finding a path. I am from having found a path. I am from losing my path. I am from finding my path again. I am from having no path to find.

I am from a time long past.

I am from the present.

I am from the future.

I am from everywhere and am going everywhere

I am from hunter gather.

I am from earth cultivator.

I am from sower and reaper, creator and destroyer. I am from here and I am from nowhere.

I am from woman.

I am from sister.

I am from mother.

I am from father.

I am from daughter.

I am from dreamer.

I am from grief.

I am from abandonment.

I am from exclusion.

I am from inclusion.

I am from no voice, to finding my true voice. I am from speaking my truth and revealing falsehood. I am from courage and cowardice. I am from fear and courage. I am from hearing many voices. I am from recognizing my own true voice.

I am from witnessing pain and exposing its source.

I am from the roots of agency,

the cauldron of action,

the garden of justice,

the mountain of liberation,

the desert of rain,

the shores of equality,

the heaven of justice,

the hell of oppression,

the cave of innocence,

the cliffs of courage,

the river of hope,

the sky of tenderness,

the tribe of my ancestors.

the rock of my humanity,

The genesis of ART,

the art of true voice,

the art of the spirit,

the witness in empathy,

the field of hope,

the fossil of life's spiral,

the matrix of life's meaning,

the power of beauty, to make the world whole, to make the world just,

for everyone.

The Roots of Art—We Are All Connected In This Way

Homo Aestheticus: Where Art Comes From and Why (Dissanayake, 1992) has been on my reading list for a couple of years but it was not until now when the course is over (having taught this second round of Expressive Arts, Leadership, and Change) that I actually have a chance to read it. As I do, I keep looking up at my self-portrait hanging in my study. Notwithstanding the "free write" that the painting generated, I must admit, the painting continues to be a mystery to me. Where has this aboriginal woman come from? Why is she coming to me now? I have painted at least 20 self-portraits in my career as an artist. This one is by far the most evocative and in some ways most elusive to interpretation.

Dissanayake is illuminating so much of the work I have been doing in the expressive arts, and particularly this study. Her thesis helps me understand the ancient roots of the power of the arts to understand, transform, inform, and build community/unity, as (in the modern context of my work as a college professor) I use the arts to facilitate inquiry and understanding for my students to help them develop critical awareness and agency for social justice work in schools and human service settings.

As I read on, I am stunned to find a more personal understanding of the centrality of the arts in my life (and my very being) as well as in my teaching. The mystery of the self-portrait is being peeled away as I read on in Dissanayke. Almost two months after painting the portrait and creating what I refer to as a "free write," (interestingly, the "free write" morphs into an "I Am From" poem), I read this.

Evidence of making special appears as early as 300 thousand years ago, ten times earlier than the cave paintings in France and Spain that (being on a grand scale and astonishing quality) are usually considered to mark the beginnings of "art." In a number of sites from that long ago, and consistently thereafter, pieces of red ochre or hematite have been found associated with human dwellings, often far from the areas in which they naturally occur. It is thought that these minerals were brought to dwelling sites to be used for coloring and marking bodies and utensils, just as people continue to do today. (Dissanayake, 1992, p. 96)

This portrait reveals to me a primal woman for whom "making special" is a way of being, as necessary and integral as her understanding of what plants to eat and what clouds precede what kind of weather. Painting her body and spying and adorning herself with fossils for their special-ness and beauty give her a sense of power in an unpredictable world, a sense of order, a sense of place, and another way of knowing. She is nomadic, the landscape is her home and as she moves through it, she is alert to small and large changes around her and responds to these changes from a strong place within herself. These skills bring *pleasure* as much as they protect and assure *survival* (Disssanayake, 1992).

It is almost as if Dissanayake is speaking about the aboriginal woman in my self-portrait when she says.

Archaeologists and anthropologists describe other behavior in humans . . . that can better be described as recognizing specialness or making special than it can be described as anything else. Wandering Mousterian hominids, for example, apparently spotted, picked up, and took with them "curios," such as unusual fossils or rocks, concretions or pyrites…exotic materials like shells and special serpentinite were transported to human occupation sites from over a hundred

140

kilometers distance and make into beads for clothing. (Dissanayake, 1992, p. 97)

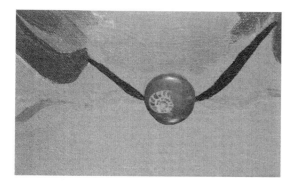

Figure 5.13. Close-up of necklace.

I look at the fossil that hangs around the neck of the aboriginal me in the self-portrait and I'm overwhelmed by what I have just read. It all makes so much sense. The connections are limitless. The self-portrait becomes the keystone of the autobiographical process that I started last year as I worked on my first Independent study. It places my beginnings and the roots of my art for justice work even earlier than I had imagined. These roots trace not just back to my early years as a child of Italian Gypsies who could not find a place to live in Brooklyn, as I originally thought, but back even farther to my ancestral human roots. This primitive woman has manifested herself now to remind me of the essential human primacy and necessity of art for all human endeavors.

According to Dissanayake, this essential human primacy and necessity is innate in all of us. As I read student journals, I am struck by how many students are frightened by the "arts." Many of them feel that the arts are for special people to create and appreciate, but not for them. I realize that, before I can teach students to use the arts to identify, explore, and address social justice issues, I have to first appreciate how strong their fear of the arts can be and why. My job is to help my students deconstruct the "art as elite activity for a few" paradigm. I believe the best way to do this is by facilitating art-making as a *process and dialogue* action as opposed to art-making to *produce a*

141

work of art or *product*. In this way, I believe I can help my students rediscover, recover, and remember the role of the arts in their own lives as a source of power and empowerment, a discovery and leadership tool, and birthright to be reclaimed. Perhaps this is why when my students experience the creative process in this way (once they get past their fears) they report a sense of the *spiritual*. Perhaps a rebirth of an essential human (necessary) behavior is for them equivalent to a *spiritual reawakening*.

Processing a multitude of mini-epiphanies, I realize it was the painting, the self-portrait and the poetry that followed that triggered many of them. Of all the authors in *Provoked by Art: Theorizing Arts-Informed Research*, Neilsen (2004) sums up my process best.

> Inquiry and knowing are expansive, difficult, passionate, catalytic. . . . Aesthetic work opens us up, opens a space that interrupts the ordinary. It forces change-ours and others'. Such open spaces . . . connect us to the human condition in a primeval way. These are spiritual dimensions, although we seldom use words like spirit, heart, and soul in the academy. The soul seeks pleasure in the purity of the esthetic experience-one in the many, many in the one. Inspirited work is necessary: heart and soul give inquiry its life. (Neilsen, 2004, p. 47)

As I examine my process as social justice educator, allowing myself "open spaces" to explore my experiences, past, present, and future, I feel I am reenacting a very ancient process of understanding and making meaning of my experience.

Finding Home: A Map to Finding My True Voice

As I related in the first part of this autoethnography (see Barbera, independent learning project, 2006b), my family was homeless in New York City for many years in my early childhood. Fourth Avenue, in Brooklyn represents for me a time of stability (not sure about that word because many things remained unstable) for my family, but stable in terms of having a place to live. The photos of Fourth Avenue (below) discovered by my older brother this summer are treasured windows on the past.

Figure 5.14. 7825 4th Avenue, spring 1955 with my mother.

Our apartment was on the third floor of the apartment building just out of the snapshot to my mother's right—apartment C3. I was overcome with emotion when I saw the photos because in these two snapshots so much history (my story) can be seen. In the photo above, my mother is the central figure in the landscape (such as it is). She is adjusting my Easter bonnet (hand-made by her). I'm about five years old in the picture. My older sister, Laura, is pulling up her sock. My younger brother, Jack, behind her is buttoning his jacket. It's all happening on Fourth Avenue, Easter Sunday morning, 1955. We are on our way to church. Seven other children are most likely running around behind the photographer, and so cannot be seen in the photo.

Figure 5.15. 7825 4th Avenue, summer 1956 (me in white dress with my father and four of my siblings).

The reason Fourth Avenue represents "home" is because it is the place where I lived the longest. Before Fourth Avenue my family experienced homelessness and dispossessions. For 10 years, Fourth Avenue was our constant home. We finally left "home" because we owed too many months back rent and so were, inevitably, ultimately, dispossessed. The true significance of Fourth Avenue is this: not before or since Fourth Avenue, have I lived in a place half . . . no, a quarter as long as I did there.

One of the assignments I gave my students this summer was to develop a multi-modal map to finding their true voice (Shapiro, 2004). In keeping with my resolve to take on myself as many of my students' assignments as possible, I decided to use the 7825 4th Avenue photo to start the "map to finding my true voice," (finding the place I belong, finding a home?).

It was on Fourth Avenue that I first became conscious of "sense of place," of earth. It was in the soil behind the green hedges in front of the building (which can be partially seen just to my mother's right in the first photo and a much better view over my father's right shoulder in the second photo) that I sunk my spoon, digging deeper and deeper, over and over, in the same hole, only to have it refilled by the building superintendent and my mother informed of my vandalism. The smell of the earth, the deeper and deeper I dug, the damper it became, the color changing to red (what we called "first" dirt or "Indian" dirt). I was absorbed for hours, faintly aware of the world

144

passing by just in front of the hedge while I and often my younger brother and sister dug our holes undetected.

Lest one think this was my only experience of "nature" as a child, I should add that we did take trips to Coney Island, Brighten Beach, and Far Rockaway. The shore and Atlantic Ocean were most present in my life. Oddly, my parents preferred heading to the beach at sunset. We would pass streaming bumper-to-bumper traffic, watching sunburned travelers on the other side of the highway, heading home from a day at the beach, as we glided along, traffic free, heading toward it. My father would set us to work gathering driftwood and set up a campfire, Gypsy style, and cook us dinner— usually chicken or hot dogs. Once dinner was over, my father set boundaries around the campfire 10 paces out, with stones that we were not to go beyond, while my parents were away, and he and my mother headed for the darkness of the ocean towards the rocks to harvest mussels to bring home with us. While my brothers and sisters played tag, the multi-colored lights from the concessions on the boardwalk flickered on the ocean to the echo of distant music and the wind picked up the smell of salt and fish. As the self-appointed keeper of the fire, I sat quietly praying that my mother and father would return soon safely to land.

I look back on the last couple of pages and realize that my map to finding my true voice is quite detailed. The process I am following here is very intuitive. I am telling a story and the story is telling me what I need to know to go on. Is this what I am supposed to be doing in an autoethnography? Am I over-indulging in my own story? Is this story seminal to my study? Does this story mean anything to anyone but me? Does it matter?

Again, the book I am reading, *Provoked by Art: Theorizing Arts-Informed Research*, comes to the rescue. I read Tracy Luciani (2004) and take heart.

> I want to tell a story that reveals the roots of my inquiry: the ways in which concepts, issues and interests interconnect; the ways in which taste, texture and tempo resonate with purpose, content, process and form, asking me: Why am I doing this? What am I unearthing? How do I dig? How do I present this? (p. 40)

I feel heartened by Luciani's words and decide to continue to map my journey home, to my true voice. I will need more visual material for my map. In late fall, I give my son, Alexander, an assignment. I have made a list of all 17 places I have lived in the last 27 years since moving to upstate New York a year before he was born. Of course, Alexander lived with me in all but the last four of these, prior to leaving home, so knows them all well. I commission him to photograph the places I have lived and he willingly takes on the (paid) assignment. Alexander studied photography while at Bard College and thrives on assignments like these.

As I upload the photos from Alexander's first day of shooting, he tells me of his adventures in going to our past dwellings. They included people who welcomed him into their homes when he revealed the nature of his task and former landlords who could hardly believe this dark-bearded, wild-haired man was the little blonde bombshell they remembered. Alexander seemed charged with energy and said, "You know, I think the land and landscapes around the house are just as important as the house. Don't you"?

With that, Alexander touched the essential purpose of the assignment. I wanted to revisit not only the dwelling, but the sense of place the surrounding landscape offered and had asked him to include shots of the surrounding landscape for that reason. I knew he really "got it" by the quality of the photos. The upload completed, I handed him back the card. He put it back in the camera and promised to do all remaining locations the following weekend. "No," he said with an incongruent smile, when I asked him if he wanted to stay for dinner, "I don't think I'll stay for dinner. I'm totally exhausted. This sure took a lot out of me," he said going out the door. It seems to have given him a lot, as well. Unwittingly, Alexander had been brought into the process of "looking back" which I believe, (as it did for my students and for me), brought him more fully into the present with empathy, toward himself and toward me as well.

Alexander finished the shoot this weekend. Photos of the landscape are even more beautiful than his first batch of photos. Over dinner to celebrate my 57th birthday, with his dad and I and our current respective partners, he reminded us that he has six more places to shoot if he decides to continue documenting places lived for himself (where he lived concurrently with his dad while he was growing up), and six more since he has been on his own. Clearly, Alexander has been cursed/blessed with his mother's Gypsy blood. Before leaving the restaurant, Alexander gives me a gift. A landscape he painted me for my birthday.

Figure 5.16. House on Calamar Lane, Woodstock.

This house on Calamar Lane, in Woodstock was the first house my son's dad and I lived in when we moved to upstate New York in 1980. I was 30 years old. This is where we lived when my son, Alexander was born in 1981.

Figure 5.17. Open meadows across the Mill Stream.

There were open meadows with views of the Catskills just across the Mill Stream (the real one, as in the song, "not the brook but the stream") and through the woods at the back of the house.

Figure 5.18. House on Wittenberg Road.

After Alexander was born, we spent a very short time in this house on Wittenberg Road until we finished fixing up the Pine Hill cottage where we were planning to live, in exchange for caretaking a large property, whose owners wanted to develop as a Yoga Center. Alexander's father still lives in the Wittenberg house today and is one of my closest friends.

Figure 5.19. Pine Hill cottage on Birch Creek Road.

This is the Pine Hill cottage on Birch Creek Road. You can see Birch Creek in the right bottom of the photo. The house had no running water, so we ran hoses from a mountain spring on the other side of the creek which gravity fed water to the house. In the winter, the line would often freeze because it was above ground. We would haul hundreds of yards of hosing into the cottage to thaw it out. It was worth it though, with a newborn baby, running water was essential.

Figure 5.20. Rosendale house on Mountain Road.

The Birch Creek Cabin was at least a half hour by car to anywhere so after plans for the Yoga Center fell through and living there for two years, we moved to the house above. The Rosendale house on Mountain Road was situated on the end of the Swangunk Ridge, which was created in the last ice age. The house was surrounded by boulders from the ridge.

Figure 5.21. Mountian Road, Rosendale.

Figure 5.22. Cabin we lived in after I split up with Alexander's father.

This is where Alexander and I lived after I split up with his dad. The landscape around the cabin was filled with magical stones and waterways. Alexander hunted

150

salamanders under rocks in the forest and released them all upon retuning home from our walks.

Figure 5.23. Magical, mystical stone croppings in the woods behind the cabin.

Figure 5.24. Leopard carved into front door.

151

Alexander and I moved across the street to a converted chicken coop with more space when a friend and my mother (on a more permanent basis) came to live with us. A leopard was carved into the front door by an artist friend and greeted all visitors with curiosity and caution. (Photo above)

Figure 5.25. Second converted chicken coop.

We went from one converted chicken coop to another a few miles away in an effort to find a better school district for Alexander (I told myself). It was my friend's idea to move.

Figure 5.26. Hearts Content Road place with footbridge.

We moved to Heart's Content Road. There was a waterfall right outside the back door. The house was accessible only by footbridge over the falls.

Figure 5.27. Falls behind Hearts Content Road house.

Our 90-year-old neighbor told us about finding arrowheads along the river and under the falls when he was a boy. Alexander and I kept our eyes always peeled but never did find one.

Figure 5.28. Along the river behind Hearts Content Road house.

Figure 5.29. Porch, meadow, and Alexander and I at Crispell Road home.

When the owner decided to sell the Waterfall House, we moved again. Our house on Crispell Road, in Olivebridge was framed by an open meadow on the back which is seen in this shot of the house. This photo of Alexander and I was taken on the porch and shows the meadow behind us. At the front of the house was a quarry, if we followed the path through the woods. We rented this house from friends and when they, too, decided to sell the house, we moved to Ohayo Mountain Road.

Figure 5.30. Ohayo Mountain Road house.

Again, my friend and partner was not happy with the tight quarters, so we traveled east across the Hudson River to the School House in Rhinebeck. It was here that Alexander painted his first major painting and declared himself an artist.

Figure 5.31. Alexander's first major painting, 1994.

Figure 5.32. School house in Rhinebeck.

I remember talking to the guidance counselor at Alexander's new school in Rhinebeck and asking him about Gifted and Talented Programs for Alexander. He looked at me rather haughtily and said, "All of our programs, Ms. Barbera, are Gifted

157

and Talented, because all of our students are gifted." Alexander finally found friends to whom he could relate. He helped start a theater group and took up guitar.

Ultimately, the rent at the School House was raised significantly the second year we lived there, so we moved into the small hamlet of Rhinecliff about a mile north of the School House.

Figure 5.33. Apartment and studio a mile north of the school house.

The storefront on the street level served as my studio and the apartment just above it is where Alexander and I lived with my partner. Alexander mostly stayed in my studio, which had a large bedroom and bath at the back. He used the bedroom window to exit the studio, undetected at night, and hang out with his friends one block away on the shores of the Hudson River. When my ten-year relationship ended and my partner moved out of the upstairs apartment, Alexander and I lived only in the studio, which fortunately had a kitchen. My sadness at the end of my relationship was equal to my sense of liberation: I would be making my own decisions about my life from this point forward.

Figure 5.34. House at 7 Charles Street.

Alexander and I moved around the corner, to 7 Charles Street, when the owners of the studio decided to sell the building to the U.S. Post Office. The storefront had been the site of the original post office in post-revolutionary war times and they wanted to restore it as such. The firehouse and church behind the Charles Street house (see Figure 5.32) provided predictable, as well as unpredictable sounds of sirens blaring and bells tolling, which, along with the AmTrak train whistles, tug boat horns on the river, and the sounds of the constant migration of birds along the river, made for a very interesting auditory experience.

This was the last house where Alexander and I lived together. Shortly after moving there, Alexander applied for early admission to Simon's Rock College, in Great Barrington, Massachusetts, an hour and a half away, and then, the following year, transferred to Bard—which was on the river a few miles away. Within one year, my ten-year relationship ended, my mother passed away, and my son left for college. My sense of identity and purpose were completely challenged. I felt . . . totally abandoned.

Painting the "Farewell" painting (see Figure 5.33) was part of my self-therapy and helped me process all of the losses I had sustained. The hawk seen just below the arch represents Alexander, perched and ready to take flight, the black and white angel wing to the left of the arch, represents my mother, and the figure below it, my partner. I stand in the foreground with my back to the viewer approaching a threshold into my future.

Figure 5.35. Farewell, 1997.

Figure 5.36. Studio at 22 Stuyvesant Street.

When Alexander left for Bard, he left home for good and I moved back across the river to economize. I took a studio in a beautiful Victorian federalist-style building at 22 Stuyvesant Street, in Kingston (see Figure 5.34). Again, I lived one block from the Hudson River as I had in Rhinecliff—only now I was on the west side of the river.

Figure 5.37. Rifton house on Hardenburgh Road.

Two years later, my new love and I decided to live together and moved into the Rifton House on Hardenburgh Road. One summer day from the porch on the left I noticed something moving in the tall grass. A short while later, a mountain lion cub poked his head up and looked at me and immediately afterwards its sibling did the same.

Figure 5.38. Stream behind Rifton house.

161

A small stream ran behind the house and it attracted many critters, but the mountain lion cubs were by far the most exotic species I had seen there. I lived in the Rifton House for nearly two years, but ultimately, I decided I much rather live on my own. I realized that I had entered this relationship prematurely. I still needed more time on my own. I had not really found my authentic voice or a place to call home.

Figure 5.39. House at 3 Charles Street, Rhinecliff.

My journey took me back across the Hudson River to Rhinecliff and to the house just next door to the last house I had lived in on Charles Street (to the left in Figure 5.37). The blue house in the center of Figure 5.37 is 3 Charles Street. I lived there alone for two years. I realized that this was really the first time I was voluntarily alone in my entire life. The last time had been by default. I had gone from living with my family of origin, to living with my sister when I left home and the both of us were in college, to having my own family, to living with a partner. And, of course, from the time he was born to when he left home after college, Alexander was at the center of my life. So this was a very big step for me.

162

I think the reason I choose to return to Rhinecliff was because I really felt at home there. All the sights and sounds were familiar and comforting to me. A very critical step in finding my true voice!

Currently, I share a home with my partner. We have a house in Woodstock, on Zena Road, on the banks of the Sawkill River, surrounded by the Catskill Mountains.

Figure 5.40. House in Woodstock and Sawkill River, 2007.

Looking back on the last 27 years has been exhausting and illuminating. I am trying to make sense of my journey as I assemble it as whole, rather then experiencing it as disparate scattered pieces of memory and time. As I think about it, I realize that I initiated only 7 of the 17 moves I made. Three were a result of house owners deciding to sell rather than rent. The other moves were initiated by my partner. The last six moves, however, were of my own initiative; although, it appears to have taken me quite some time to find my voice in the matter.

But, as I drill down and explore this experience other more complex themes appear—some very personal and some universal. Issues of childhood imprinting (the culture of my parents' belief in the nomadic way of life as necessary for survival), internalization of the American culture's gender bias, single parenthood, financial frailty, dependency, interdependency, and responsibility for the care of my ailing mother all help make sense of my years of wandering and hopefully contextualize the tableaux for the observer.

What sustained me throughout this migration/uprooting/settling/migration pattern was the land—the landscape was my escape. Finding my place and peace in the landscape was the way I grounded myself. The beauty and constancy-in-change of the natural world gave me strength in the face of frequent change and living with uncertainty. The path to finding my voice involved letting go of so much, cycling between clinging and letting go, fear and courage, love and abandonment, despair and faith (in myself), confusion and clarity, powerlessness and self-empowerment, and finally between dependency and sovereignty over my own life.

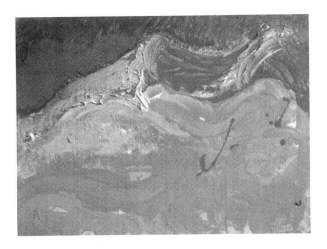

Figure 5.41. Catskill Mountains, 2007.

Figure 5.42. Alexander and I at 676 Zena Road, 2006.

Epilogue to the Map

Twice in the last year, my partner has asked me to move away with him. The first time he wanted to move to California to be closer to his aging mother. The second time he wanted to move to Vermont to be closer to his spiritual teacher. Both times I declined (not without much anguish over the possibility of losing someone very important to me). After all I have experienced, I am clear about where I want to be right now and that is exactly where I am—a place with family, community, and meaning for me! As of today, my partner and I are still together, and last November was the beginning of my third year living here on the banks of the Sawkill River, setting a new record.

As I reflect on my process, I realize in a new way the value of autobiographical self-study. I realize that one of the most important things I gained from this process was self-empathy (not sympathy). I have been able to put self-judgment aside and reframe the past from my position in the present in a more gentle way. I imagine something similar happening for my students as they journey back and look at the events in their lives. Perhaps the value of this type of time travel moves us to develop that "unappreciated way of being" (Rogers, 1980) that is so essential in any work for social justice. Perhaps the empathy gained through the autobiographical process reorients the compassionate heart so it may join with the critical mind to more effectively work for justice.

When I wrote my first essay for the Leadership and Change Program, I remember deliberately leaving out my early experience of homelessness. The shame and pain was still with me then and I did not want to expose myself or reopen those feelings again. For my organizational change project, I designed an Expressive Arts Training Program for homeless shelter staff in my county. Taken all together, it is no surprise in light of this journal, that in all of the different professional roles I have had over the last 30 years, I have been advocating for children and families. In retrospect, it appears as if I may have been moving closer to revealing to others the primary justice issues of my own life, but it was not until now that I feel I have actually brought my past and present consciously into alignment. In many ways, I believe that this is the alignment that my students must be experiencing when they do their own self-identity work through the arts: a courageous alignment of past and present for direction, focus, and commitment (professional and personal) for future work in the world.

Mask and Poem (Revisited)

Figure 5.43. Mask "Home."

My mask explored the polarities of Home and Homelessness. Images of a white wolf, buttercups, hawk, and snake represent allies for me, helping me find my place in nature, feel comfortable in the natural world, and experience it as HOME.

166

The following poem was written last year during my study of the Gypsy (Romani) culture in relation to my culture of origin. It was not included in my autoethnographic journal last year but has its roots on 4th Avenue, so I am including it here. It harkens back to my experiences starting on 4th Avenue, up to the present. The poem was my way of making sense of my life's events in relation to my family of origin.

Sisters

Inside a Holocaust rages,
Burning families of Gypsies alive.
This place has sister
Pitted against sister-
One turning the other in,
A black hole of betrayal.

Each unsure of what really happened
What really started this sad state of affairs.
Tenderly, in unison,
They peek at the wound.
But, oh, it's not a wound after all—
Wait, stop. . . .
It's a beating heart, still.

Inside a war rages,
Killing future sisters,
Night star-gazers,
Rooftop sun-set watchers.
But if this sister pair perish,
What hope do other sisters have?

Barbed wire encircles the camp.
The brutal night descends on their dwelling places.

167

(Safety in numbers is their only hope.)

Your father, grandfather and his father before him
Were called "murderer."
Will one more murder matter?
Will one outlive the other?
And, without the other,
Can either really live?

Remembering her multi-colored gypsy skirt
Swaying hips, finger tips,
Michelangelo angel face,
Lover of shells,
Lover of love—
Winter of pain. . . .

The Holocaust rages on,
Inferno's mind (that)
Can not forget

Can not forgive,
Must not remember
The hunger,
The whacked, knife-wielding brother—
Ropes—
Dissections, roach poisoned dreams.
His tainted touch,
Tainting innocence.

Sisters tending,
Pretending to love
But not really knowing how.
Perhaps one day they'll truly know.
Liberation grown

On generations of lies.

Gypsy eyes, disguised,

But free.

Self-Study Research and Social Justice Education

Suominen (2006), a social justice education researcher, feels that, as a social justice educators, engaging in self-study and exposing our multi-dimensional lives to our students is essential for authentic learning to result. She encourages educators to teach "who they are" (Goodson & Numan, 2002). The following quote from her autoethnographic journal, titled, "Teaching," encapsulates the essence of her goal to teach equity, critical awareness, acceptance, and understanding of diversity through the arts.

> You have met them in the space between you and them, because if you don't . . . there is no learning, only memorizing. You have to reveal yourself to your students, because if you don't, they won't believe you. If I want to teach, for me, for the teacher, the option of staying anonymous doesn't exist. (Suominen, 2006, pp. 151-152)

Bullough and Pinnegar's (2001) criteria for quality self-study echoes Suominen's metaphor of the "space between" as a mediating space, between self-study per se, and the real job of quality self-study research. Bullough and Pinnegar articulate what self-study researchers need to consider in order to have a balanced research in this way.

> While self-study researchers acknowledge the role of the self in the research project. . . . Such study does not focus on the self per se, but on the space between self and the practice engaged in. There is always a tension between those two elements, self and the arena of practice, between self in relation to practice and the others who share the practice setting. Each self-study researcher must negotiate that balance, but it must be a balance—tipping too far toward the self side produces solipsism or a confessional, and tipping too far the other way turns self-study into traditional research. (2001, p. 15)

My intention in this autoethnographic study has been to reveal my process as I attempt to describe my journey as I mirror the processes that I ask my students to employ in their study of social justice pedagogy, in the Expressive Arts, Leadership, and Change course. My hope is that the balance between "self and the arena of

169

practice" that Bullough and Pinnegar (2001) recommend, I have achieved. Judging from my students' responses in interviews and self-learning and evaluation papers, as well as in the quotes in this final section, I believe I have.

Closing—Retrospective Show

Figure 5.44. Students and I set up Retrospective Show, 2007.

Along with my students, I set up an exhibition of my expressive artwork for the Retrospective. There is a hush, everyone is very busy, and a sense of reverence pervades the space.

Figure 5.45. Students viewing exhibit of my work at the Retrospective Show, 2007.

The Retrospective Show began with students reading their "I Am From" poems and ended with each student leaving a short note at each person's exhibit. My suggestion was to leave a message, as a gift to the artist, briefly describing how they felt emotionally after viewing each student's exhibit.

I'll end my autoethnographic journal with my students' responses to my exhibit. Some were signed and some were anonymously gifted.

Wow! Wow! To your creativity, poetry, spirituality, generosity, and survival. (C.C.)

I truly appreciate how comfortable you are expressing yourself to your class.

Inspirational! Your class has taught me so much. However, your energy, spirituality, and dedication taught me even more.

Very powerful and what an amazing journey.

Powerful, inspiring, creative. Truly an inspiration. (K.P.)

Visually stunning.

Inspiring, strong, colorful, magical. Thank you.

Lucy, beautiful history, roots, sisters poem—so moving. Thank you. (J.D.)

Thank you for being a part of my path and teaching me the way to happiness. You are beautiful.

It's obvious—your voice, your ancestry—a lesson for me!

Lucy, *You are a priest among us!* Your spirit comes through in your art and being. Your soul, as your art, is essential. (J.B.)

Lucy, I love the pictures! Wow, your sisters poem really touched my heart.

Lucy, Would I, could I ever reach your dimension of creativity. Thank you for such inspiration. (G.S.)

Professor, Your work is amazing! You make me happy. You make me feel my inner self. You are positive and help me find the spiritual. You bring peace. I needed this class. Thank you. (L.O.)

Lucy, thanks for inviting us all back. Already it feels like a soul/spirit/revival/reunion! (C.M.) (All quotes 7-28-07)

Next Steps

My two studies dovetailed, weaving both content and methods and have provided me with new understanding, appreciation, integration, and application of the expressive arts for social justice teacher education and leadership for change and catapulted me into new directions and questions. When designing my second study, I introduced a visit to an art museum on campus for my opening class. One of my objectives for doing this was to assist students in overcoming their fear of art by breaking down the walls, which they and others have built over the course of their lives that separate them from art and the art-making process. Over the last 12 years of teaching expressive arts, I had heard students repeatedly say things like, "I am not an artist. I can't make art. I am afraid of art. I don't understand art." These sentiments have not changed in the last couple of years that I have been teaching Expressive Arts, Leadership, and Change, but, in many ways, appear to have intensified.

My ultimate goal as a social justice teacher educator is to give teachers expressive arts-based pedagogical tools to utilize in their schools or human service settings to identify, explore, and address social justice issues. If I don't address the fear (and resistance) factor that many of my students, themselves, encounter upon entering my course, how will my students be able to anticipate, understand, and work with this strong emotion in their own attempts to use the *palpable pedagogy* of the expressive arts in their teaching for social justice? I feel the two studies that I have undertaken have led me to this very important question and to the next steps of my study.

I think that all true leadership is indeed spiritual leadership, even if you hardly ever hear it put that flatly. The reason is that beyond everything else that can be said about it, leadership is concerned with bringing out the best in people. As such, one's best is tied intimately to one's deepest sense of oneself, to one's spirit. My leadership efforts must touch that in myself and in others. (Vaill, 1989, pp. 223-224)

This summer, I will be teaching Expressive Arts, Leadership, and Change for the third time. As a humanistic educator, my goal is to bring the best out in my students, to bring them together, and to bring them to a higher place in their personal development and professional practice. To achieve this, I believe I will have to address (their) fear of the arts, first by supporting students through their fear, by exposing fear as a phenomenon and bringing it consciously to light, and then by understanding its function and its power over the creative impulse. It is a goal worthy of a "mindful" researcher (Bentz & Shapiro, 1998) and will constitute the final phase of my research for my book.

173

Figure 5.46. Buddha of No Fear.

When I packed all of the learning materials to take to the opening day of class of Expressive Arts, Leadership, and Change, I looked up and noticed the *Buddha of No Fear* on my mantle, reached up, took it down, and tucked it into my computer bag. I was going to meet a new group of students and was determined to address the issue of *fear of art* with this group openly and consciously. My intention was to expose fear and examine its dimensions. I knew it would be no small feat and so I would need all the help I could get. Buddha would be my ally and protector (and, as it turned out, the class mascot). An account of my students' experience of fear, its impact on them, their response to it, and my learning about their fear of art is chronicled in chapter 4 of this study.

It is the subtext or antenarrative (Boje, 2001), the culture of my inner self that will be the main focus of this brief, final section of my three-year autoethnographic journal. It will be a *tabla rasa* for my personal journey, my inner emotional life, a place to capture the culture of the person inside the person teaching the course and, as such, a place to pay homage to my brother, Tom.

Figure 5.47. Opening Day of Class—July 12, 2008, Tom's Birthday

I am at the college early to set up and organize the class materials. The weekend was an emotional one. My family members (25 in all) and I had gathered at the South Street Seaport to take the Staten Island Ferry loop from Manhattan to Staten Island and back. This was to be our "east coast" memorial for Tom. As we passed the Statue of Liberty, each of us took some his ashes from the urn and scattered them into the river, just as we had done with my sister, Joyce's ashes 10 years before. This was our way of letting him go, of liberating him. This was very hard for me to do, even symbolically.

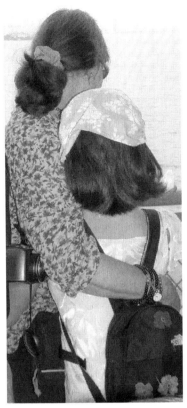

Figure 5.48. My niece, Jackie Joy and I releasing Tom's ashes.

Loss and Change

On February 13, 2008, I received a call that would change my world. The call was from my 20-year-old nephew, Tommy Jr., breaking the difficult news to me in the most sensitive and loving way that his dad, my brother Tom, my true friend, had been killed in a car crash in California, just a block from his home. As I write, some of the shock that has insulated me from the hammering pain of loss over the last several months has now worn off and I am left with a very deep sadness, remembering my loss of Tom. The process I used to work through my grief was art-making through collage and poetry. I took printouts of old emails Tom had sent me and some photos and created a collage-homage to him. I am amazed at how such totally random email messages were able to provide such deep insight into the person that Tom was.

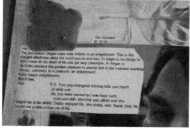

Figure 5.49. Close-ups of Homage to Tom, collage, 2008.

From the very beginning of my doctoral studies, Tom had been someone with whom I could share every aspect of my work. He was intellectually, physically, and spiritually AWAKE! Tom was just as excited about what I was learning, researching, and applying as I was. The Sunday before Tom died, we talked on the phone, as we did just about every weekend. I read him an excerpt from my second "I Am From" poem cited earlier in this autoethnographic journal. Tom was a child and family therapist working for a county social services agency in northern California. He had begun to use many of the expressive arts processes I shared with him with his clients, made up of families, children, and mostly men, who, because of their violent actions towards their families, were court-mandated to enter therapy. In fact, he invited the men in his men's group to write their own "I Am From" poems after reading them mine. He reported that it was a cathartic experience for them, with many of them weeping and comforting one another. Tom said, "Lu, I am starting to really 'get' what you're all about now. I am realizing more and more that *life* is art and that every person is *a work of art.*" We were both silent, each at our end of the phone, separated in space by 3,000 miles, but totally connected in this truth and our love and appreciation of each other. This truth

177

was the healing energy he brought to his clients. This was the healing he brought to his own life, and his gift to me was his belief in me and my work of using the arts to honor life and help alleviate suffering in the world.

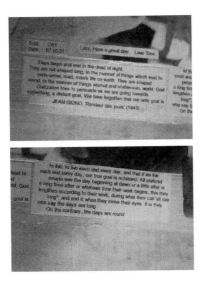

Figure 5.50. Homage collage, close-ups, 2008.

In January 2007, Tom had attended my final residency in Seattle to experience firsthand, my Antioch learning community, giving him a more complete picture of my doctoral experience. Tom was so much a part of my experience that I could not imagine writing this autoethnographic journal without acknowledging him and how much I do now, and will in the future, miss him. The path forward will be bittersweet. Each time I imagined myself presenting my dissertation and graduating, Tom was always prominently in the picture. He will not be with me (in body) when I do, or on the road ahead, but I know he will be with me in spirit as he always has been and this will have to be my only consolation as I continue the amazing journey of life and *becoming* a reflective scholar, practitioner—able to imagine and lead change.

Figure 5.51. Close-ups, Homage collage, 2008.

The Altar I Have Made of You

I light a lamp on the altar I have made of you.
You are reaching out to me—anyone—
Looking at your reaching hand
I reach for the place that you inhabit.
Habituated—I return throughout the night
Reaching for you—
Knowing in an oceanic way
That you are within reach—
Felt—but yet still unseen.
Spirit Brother, you ARE.
You touch the ground of love
And I, (awaken, a beggar),
The ground for hope.
3-21-09

Figure 5.52. Touchstone for Tom, hawk feather and fox tooth, 2008.

In The Hours You Are Me

In *Dreamtime,* the once-living and the living
Walk hand in hand,
Talk in intelligible tongues.
 In *Dreamtime,* your morning trees
Are sprouting ice flowers.
They melt-smelt into glass
Venetian flowers.
Hours are milliseconds to you,
Kaliugas (millennia) to me—
And time's twin
Is your hourglass
Looking directly into my mirrored
eyes—cries and lies.
Tell me, Brother, what ancient or modern
Or future laws guide you now?
Tell me the moon is a star.
Tell me your are laughter—

I hear it

In the hours you are me—dreaming

You are me

Dreaming . . .

3-21-09

Figure 5.53. Tom in turban, Chico, California, 2008.

I am from Tom.

I am from knowing him.

I am from loving him.

I am from his loving me.

I am from understanding him.

And him me.

I am from his deep brown eyes

Reflected in my deep brown eyes.

I am from his hurts.
I am from his joy.
I am from his intellect.
I am from his compassion.
I am from his sensitivity.

I am from his howling hurts.
I am from his deep old wounds.
I am from his despair.
I am from his despondency.
I am from his depression.

I am from his recovery of himself.
I am from his personhood.
I am from his integrity.
I am from his towering spirit.
I am from his colossus of being and feeling.
I am from the depth of his character and personhood.

I am from his love of beauty.
I am from his searching.
I am from his searching for the Divine.
I am from his searching for love.
I am from his always thinking he had found it
In the face and form of a young woman.
I am from his longing for fulfillment.
I am from his longing for love and acceptance.

I am from his catharsis.
I am from his generosity.
I am from his self-forgiveness.
I am from his roots.

I am from his wings of desire and yearning.

I am from his search for the Grail.
I am from his devotion to the Dharma Padma.
I am from his love of the Ruba'iyat of Omar Khayyam.
I am from his "lock, leaf, and door" of Thomas Wolfe.
I am from his love of the Path.

I am from his innocence.
I am from his worldliness.
I am from his simplicity.
I am from his complexity.
I am from his compassion.
I am from his beginning.
I am from his never-ending.

I am from his desperation.
I am from his rage.
I am from his contradictions.
I am from his constancy
I am from his wild nature.
I am from his love of nature.
I am from his tender caring.
I am from his dark introversion
And his magnanimous extroversion.

I am from his courage.
I am from his wisdom.
I am from his fear.
I am from his bellow.
I am from his roar.
I am from his silence.
I am from his solitude.
I am from his solicitude.

I am from his solace.

I am from his honor.

I am from his humor and his raucous laughter.

I am from his calling me up at 5:00 a.m. Sunday mornings and saying: "Hey, Lu"!

I am from his blame.

I am from his shame.

I am from his whisper.

I am from his shared secrets.

I am from his lies.

I am from his truth.

I am from his yoga.

I am from his turban.

I am from his walks in the canyons.

I am from his lock of hair.

I am from his tender caring

I am from his loving glance.

I am from his love and pride in his son.

I am from his father.

I am from his mother.

I am from his childhood.

I am from his adolescence.

I am from his adulthood.

I am from his sisters and brothers.

I am from his confusion.

I am from his delusions.

I am from his cries.

I am from his victory over fear.

I am from his commitment to justice.

I am from his generosity.

I am from his clarity.

I am from his story.
I am from his past.
I am from his present.
I am from his future.
I am from his heart.
I am from his soul.
I am from his indomitable spirit.
I am from his life.
I am from his death.
I am from his eternal hope.
I am from his mystery.

I am from him
And he is from me.
4-14-08

Figure 5.54. The healing power of love, Tommy, Jr. and I, 2008.

To be continued . . .

Chapter VI: Discussion of Conclusions

Art as Mystery

Through this study, I have come to believe that, in many ways, the arts are fundamentally a mystery, even and especially now in modern/post-modern times. Throughout recent history, much has been speculated and written about the arts and their origins, with extraordinary theories spun about arts' beginnings, purpose, and meaning. These theories are compelling, and wildly diverse. Some of these include: art as symbol or symbolic language (Jung, 1964), the function of art in the development of consciousness (Read, 1965), art as a form of associative thinking, a socio-biological process, a poetic search for meaning and understanding (Wilson, 1978, 1984), art in the bio-behavioral paradigm, as a human biological behavior, necessary for survival (Dissanayake, 1990, 1992, 2000), and art's purpose in ancient times had been considered universally to be a decorative embellishment for utilitarian objects. Theorists have created schema to map creativity hierarchically (Sternberg, 1999; Sternberg, Grigorenko, & Singer, 2004), stratifying talent, and artistic potential. Many have written about what qualifies as art, some in very thoughtful liner fashion. Dutton (2009) believes that the "characteristic features found cross-culturally in the arts can be reduced to a list of core items" (p. 51), 12 in his version.

Yet, can we really know? Can we really know definitively what art is, considering all that has been given the title *art*, over millennia and into the present time; and how often that has changed and is morphing still, even as I write about it? Can we really know every facet of every diamond in the deep diamond mine we call art? As with all sacred mysteries, it is the power of the mystery itself, that leads us, not to answers, but instead (and better still), to a deeper knowing of ourselves, our purpose, our responsibility, and our relationship in/with the world, and to a more conscious quest, a more determined path into the mystery.

Just when I think I understand art, like the shape shifter it is, it changes and reveals a new dimension—yet another unappreciated facet. My students are an example of one such facet. "But," the reader might inquire, "Is their expressive art, art? Is what they have created throughout the course beautiful? What does this discussion have to do with the topic of this paper, what, indeed, with social justice teacher education, and how does the discussion support the theory of the arts as *palpable pedagogy?*" Additionally, questions may arise in the reader about whether my students' engagement with the arts qualifies as real art.

187

The closest analogy in the art world to the expressive art produced by my students is known alternately as Outsider Art (Bottoms, 2007; Rhodes, 2000), Naïve Art (Brodskaya, 2007), and in some circles, Art Brute, meaning raw or rough art, (ugly art?)—a name given it by French artist, Jean Dubuffet, to describe art made outside of the mainstream art world. Currently, this genre of art is highlighted in a yearly festival in New York City and generates millions of dollars on the art market, displayed in the hippest art galleries and represents raw, authentic, unaffected expression. Like outsider art, my students' art is characterized by vitality, authenticity, raw energy, naïve imagery, bold color, risky juxtapositions, and creative invention. Like outsider art, my students' art seems to have been drawn from a very deep source within them, emanating from ancient creative impulses. Able to express themselves, fired by the imagination and fanned by their emotions, my students' art generated feelings, asked and answered questions, explored concerns, allowed the imagination to envision solutions, represented hopes, and met in a community of shared dreams for positive change in the world.

Does their art fall under the realm of beauty? In answer, I would point to beauty's ability to magnetize truth and justice. Scarry (1999) says it is time to stop talking about beauty in whispers and to leverage it for justice. It is beauty, she says, that "intensifies the pressure we feel to repair existing injuries" (p. 57) and "prepares us for justice" (p. 78). Art, bound to beauty, beauty to truth, and truth to justice is a powerful combination. Scarry believes that "the political rejects beauty on the grounds that it is too powerful" (p. 85). Might this be why only certain works are labeled art and only certain people (elaborately stratified and qualified) are labeled artist? Is art's power tied to its ability to reveal truth, open the imagination to what might be (Greene, 1995), and provoke action for justice? Might the need to control art's power be the reason that art at the service of beauty, truth, and justice have become marginalized as outsider manifestations? Has not art's power already been taken under the control of a few at the loss to many, to be metered out in prescribed portions, and experienced through one set prism? Has the human evolutionary need to create expressively, join in creative community, revel in the sheer pleasure of song, color, and form, and imagine ways for conscious action toward a just world been obliterated and replaced by acquisitiveness and affluence?

Kenny (1998), speaking of beauty from an ancient culture's perspective, grounds beauty and art to the earth, to life, and to individual and collective stories,

188

sensory experience, imagination, community, and change.

As First Nations peoples we experience and define beauty in relation to the way we live. Our relationship to Mother Earth and to each other, the way we live together in a place, our appreciation of holistic aspects of life all coalesce to give a sense of coherence to our worlds. It is our ability to sense this coherence that can give us the confidence to express ourselves fully, define ourselves authentically, and assist us in the creation of our own stories. Through this sense of coherence, we know who we are and we can see the visions of who we might become in the future. This visionary landscape is rich in image, metaphor, and symbol. It is punctuated by texture, song, color, story, prose. It is implied in the patterns of a basket, the shape of a carving, and reflects the lands that we inhabit, our experiences on it, and the knowledge that we acquire because of our respect for place. This is our sense of art as First Peoples. (p. 77)

In the culture Kenny celebrates, beauty and art *are* life. Her description of their cohesion gives a glimpse of the roots of art to which Dissanayake (1990, 1992, 2000) so often refers and provides us with an inkling of how completely integrated beauty, art, and life were in ancient times.

Bayles and Orland (1993) say that "In making art you declare what is important." Should this powerful vehicle for voice be afforded to a few select people and denied to others? Like Dissanayake (1990, 1992, 2000), Kenny (1998), and Read (1965), Bayles and Orland remind us of a very old and deep impulse or instinct (Dutton, 2009) at work in the creation of art. Although self-expression is an important aspect of making art, art is not simply about self-expression.

Art is something you do out in the world, or something you do about the world, or even something you do *for* the world. The need to make art may not stem solely from the need to express who you are, but from a need to complete a relationship with something outside yourself. As a maker of art you are custodian of issues larger than self. (Bayles & Orland, 1993, p. 108)

I am aligned with the paradigm of the arts as a human birthright (Dissanayake, 1992) and believe, broadly speaking, that the arts belong to and can be accessed, experienced, *and* generated by everyone. My students have confirmed this belief. Participating in an everyday form of art-making, many of my students worked through initial resistance (and sometimes substantial fear) to engage in the arts, many for the first time. By doing so, they proved that when the deep roots of art are tapped, there is a human response. For most of my students, the response was instantaneous, felt within minutes of engaging with the arts, for others it was a slower process, more akin to a somnambulist's reawakening and needing time to reassemble the splintered parts of their being into conscious cohesion. I am reminded of the oft-repeated feedback I received from so many of my students. "This class gave me a piece of myself back" (E.F., self-learning paper, 2006, p. 4). It gave them back what was already theirs, was once theirs, an act of social justice in and of itself, according to my students.

Students explored their own lives poetically and, as a result, were able to look at others compassionately and join in community to imagine and plan action for change and justice in their small piece of the world. Greene's (2007b) wish for teachers to develop compassion to create a vision of action for positive change is exactly what my students did as they engaged with the arts and created a unique culture of caring and commitment to social justice.

> I cannot but wish that practicing teachers . . . share compassion and concern, and . . . ponder ways of suffusing their teaching with visions of action, with efforts to pay heed, to change consciousness or, perhaps, hearts and minds. (pp. 1-2)

For my students, engagement with the arts was simultaneously the expressive vehicle and fertilizer of the imagination. Like the outsiders they were, their authenticity and courage were indisputable as they progressed from their first tentative poetic self-expressions to harnessing the arts to explore "issues larger than [them] selves" (Bayles & Orland, 1993, p. 108). As a result of their process, my students grasped the potential of the arts to do the same for *their* students.

In this research study, I set out to explore the culture of an arts-based social justice teacher education course, hoping to shed light on the unique culture created when the arts were employed at the service of teacher education for social justice. My purpose for the study was to learn about the culture that was generated when the arts are used to identify, explore, and address social justice issues in the context of a teacher education course, called "Expressive Arts, Leadership, and Change." Bringing together many disparate disciplines, I set out to discover how teacher education, united with social justice education and joined with the arts might support leadership and change for social justice. How these various disciplines intersected and worked to support one other, creating a unique culture, was thoroughly documented in the findings presented in chapter 4 and will be briefly reviewed again in this chapter.

190

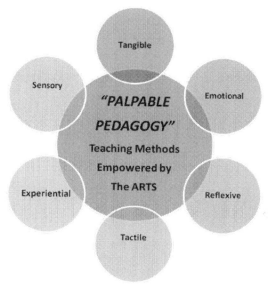

Figure 6.1. Palpable pedagogy.

On the last day of class, in the first year that I taught Expressive Arts, Leadership, and Change, I had an epiphany. The following excerpt from my journal documents my realizations on that day and the genesis of my use of the term *palpable pedagogy* to describe the generative process of teaching and learning through the arts in social justice education. The excerpt also locates in time and space the beginning of my inquiry into the culture of arts-based social justice teacher education, and my desire to shed light on what and how the arts contribute to the field of social justice teacher education.

The room is alive with a palpable energy. There is a feeling of connection and unity, of everything coming together for students. The students are sharing their "Touchstones" and as they do, I realize that the processes that I have been facilitating, teaching, and learning are *palpable pedagogy*, teaching methods that allow learning to be felt, experienced, and lived creatively. It's a critical pedagogy that is reciprocal, communal, touchable, graspable, and tangible; physically visible and emotionally felt. (Barbera, teaching journal, 2006c, p. 36)

The revelation I experienced in that moment was pivotal to my understanding of the power and empowerment of the arts to make social justice education *tangible* for my students through their *engagement* with the arts. I discovered that *palpable pedagogy* was palpable not just metaphorically, but concretely, because it was experienced and felt physically, through the senses. It was felt internally, where felt emotions could take shape nonverbally and then become concretized through the arts, in three-dimensional form. Felt emotion and idea could be *seen* and touched. Later, I would understand more completely that it was palpable or felt on these multiple levels specifically *because* it was arts-based.

Figure 6.2. Students sharing Touchstones, 2008.

What I have come to understand and appreciate through this research is that the *palpable pedagogy* that the arts provide is capable of transforming abstract concepts about social justice into concrete understanding and experience through the senses, emotion, and imagination to catalyze empathy and compassion for self and others, and build community and alliances for collaboration for social justice action in the world. Runco (2007), in his definition of imagination, underscores how the senses, as conduits of the imagination, are integrally wired to our consciousness of past, present, and future action.

192

[Imagination] is a special feature or form of human thought characterized by the ability of the individual to reproduce images or concepts originally derived from *basic senses* [italics added] but now reflected in one's consciousness as memories, fantasies or future plans. (p. 13)

Interconnecting Themes Revisited

The primary themes the data revealed were *identity, reflection, dialogue,* and *community* and these were deeply interconnected and profoundly amplified through the arts. These primary themes spawned a group of sub-themes: *emotion, compassion, fear of the arts,* and *action,* which interconnected and overlapped with the primary themes. The rich, arts-based classroom artifacts, including student assignments, photos of student artwork, video of students' learning processes, and audio of student interviews and dialogue groups revealed a multi-striated culture.

Inferences, based on the data, can be made regarding the connection between student engagement with the arts and a deepened effect on their learning about social justice. It seems clear that there was a continuum of not only extrinsic, but, just as importantly, intrinsic benefits to the students resulting from their identity exploration, verbal and nonverbal reflection, collegial dialogue, and community building through the arts. Additionally, the alchemy of the arts provoked an array of emotions, including fear of the arts, on one end of the continuum, and compassion, (which ignited the imagination with a desire to act(ion) for social justice) on the other end.

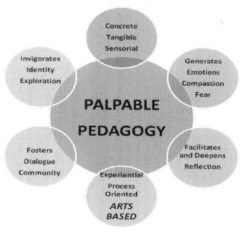

Figure 6.3. Palpable pedagogy's function and relation to themes and sub-themes.

193

Through my research, I discovered that the arts unleashed the imagination and assisted my students, in astonishing ways, to join their minds and their senses with their hearts through their own *felt, sensed,* and *lived* experiences. These experiences were recollected, activated, and deepened by students' engagement with the arts, bringing students (individually and collectively) to a deeper and often transcendent state of learning and commitment to social justice.

Figure 6.4. Past, present, and future.

I use to think photography could change the world.

Now I realize I can change the world.

The world will change little by little and so will I. (H.B., student photographic study, 2008)

Finally, through this study, I realized that the arts, as a *palpable pedagogy,* can provide educators, social change agents, and students with powerful tools to identify, examine, and address social justice issues, and to initiate positive change in the world, by tapping the ancient roots of art in post-modern times for social justice, by releasing the imagination (Greene, 1995) in the service of social justice.

Antagonists to the Arts

As I propose the use of the arts as a pedagogical tool for social justice education, I am mindful of the challenges for the practitioner of arts-based education

194

for social justice and of the many antagonists there are to the arts. Two antagonists of immediate concern to me are:

1. The diminished position of the arts in education, as a result of the educational community's fascination with the technical dimensions of education and emphasis on student assessment and measurement, and curriculum and pedagogical standardization.

2. The fear of the arts.

My first concern is political and systemic. As learning institutions are becoming more and more focused on the technical aspects of teaching and learning, the buzz words in education are now: measurable outcomes, accountability, standardization, and high stakes assessments. These assessments are on preset goals in all academic disciplines catering to students and teachers who are adept in linguistic/mathematical intelligences. This leaves those with multi-varied intelligences to be sacrificed and perish on the altar of measurable outcomes (for whom, of what, for what?). Greene (2007h) says, "Since the core emphasis of the legislation named 'No Child Left Behind' is on graded achievement, assessment, and the rest, it is difficult to believe that humanization is a central national goal" (p. 1).

Read (1965), even before the full dawning of the digital age, was concerned with the technical preoccupations of education and their threat to the importance of the senses and the aesthetic in education:

Do not muddy with erudition and vain learning those crystal fountains from which flow our most essential creative energies. Those fountains are bedded in the human frame; they are the unpolluted rivers of perception and imagination. Education should therefore be conceived as primarily a cultivation of these sensuous activities, as proposed by philosophers and poets, and if we find it difficult to accept, it is no doubt because our sensibilities are no long responsive to the original sources of human vitality and vision. (1965, pp. 138-139)

Greene (2007h) also cites the sensual as a primary aspect of the arts and couples it with the imagination, included here in her definition of aesthetics:

Aesthetics is the study of the arts: the nature of art objects, the making of art, the art (or aesthetic) experience, the relation between art and culture, the role of the perceiver, the *sensual* [italics added] and imaginative aspects of art. (p. 1)

Both Read (1965) and Greene (2007c), very much in the fine tradition of Dewey (1934), believe that the arts are "essential to life and growth of a culture"

195

(Greene, 2007c, p. 1). This study revealed a truth and challenge for all educators. Making the arts available to everyone *is* social justice.

But, pressures coming both from state and federal mandates for students to meet pre-set goals in all academic subjects have preempted the typical use of the arts in many schools. These pressures are politically and ideologically driven, catering to a business/corporate agenda. Greene (2007b) speaks about the political foe of the arts for educational change thus

> The transformation of education is no longer a merely academic matter or a matter of cheerful generalizations and clichés. It is a political struggle as much as a pedagogical struggle. And, yes, if the function of the arts is to open windows on the possible—on what might be and what ought to be—it has to be an aesthetic struggle as well. (p. 4)

It is hard to imagine the arts opening windows on the possible for students, when many are not given access to them. Viewed as non-academic and, thus, not worthy of prime time, in many schools the arts have been relegated to after school programs or to gifted and talented students, adept at verbal linguistic and/or mathematical sense-making. These students readily finish the more important academic work, earning the *privilege* to participate in the arts. Yet, other students who would benefit immensely (if not more so) from a reprieve from the technical stresses and production/product paradigm of learning are given the least access to art programs.

Does not this dynamic regarding the access to the arts mirror the critical dimensions noted in my earlier discussion in this chapter regarding who can make, appreciate, and own the arts in the dominant society? Just as Greene (2007b) calls for opening windows on the possible through the arts, Giroux (2001), calls for a radical pedagogy to create a "vision that celebrates not what is but what could be" (p. 242). Through this research, I have come to appreciate that making the arts available to everyone, students and teachers alike, as *palpable pedagogy*, is itself a form of social justice, not just an earned privilege, but a human right—simultaneously a window on the possible and a vision of what could be.

My second concern may very well, at least in part, result from my first concern and centers on the phenomenon of fear of the arts that was dazzlingly revealed through this study. If the arts are to be taken seriously as pedagogical tools for social justice teacher education, it is, first of all, necessary to make the arts readily available and valued in education. Secondly, it is critical to thoroughly understand and address the

196

fear of art. How can one hope to use the arts pedagogically for social justice teacher education, if teachers themselves are afraid of the arts? And how can teachers hope to utilize the arts to teach social justice in their classrooms, without themselves being able to anticipate, understand, and accommodate for the *fear of arts* at play in their own students and to understand the roots of that fear and how it relates to the dominant culture's relationship to the arts as power, earned entitlement, and so on. As a humanistic educator, students' affective experiences are of considerable concern and importance to me. In my view, fear is antithetical to learning and, for this reason, it is critical to address this phenomenon when arts-based pedagogical practice is being advocated.

Interestingly, fear of the arts paralleled fear of leadership for some of my students. While discussing future leadership and change action in their roles as teachers, many students shared their fear of leadership, as well. Flip chart notes from this discussion reflect this:

Essential Question: What might get in your way in a leadership role?

Fear

Fear of leadership

Fear of failure

Fear of success

Fear of judgment

Fear of change

Fear of the unknown

Fear of conflict

Fear of bureaucracy

Fear of "isms"

Fear of external voices/culture

Fear of not doing enough (2008, flip chart notes, 7-13-08)

Bayles and Orland (1993) say that "In making a piece of art, the artist and the world are changed" (pp. 105-106). If we assume, based on the results of this study and the work of Greene (1979, 1995, 2007a-h), Kenny (1982, 1989, 1998), Shapiro (2004, 2006), Eisner (1991, 2002a, 2008), and Noel (2003), that the engagement with the arts has the potential to create positive change, than it follows that overcoming the fear of the arts and experiencing them not as enemy, but ally, would be a necessary first step to harnessing their power for social justice in education.

197

How can art be used for leadership and change, if fear of art and fear of leadership is common among teachers?

When I asked my students what would assist them in getting past their fear, they said:

Saying "no" to hierarchies

Trusting myself

Education

Shedding limitations

Commitment

Experience

New vision

Hope (2008, flip chart notes, 7-13-08)

As we saw in chapter 4, in confronting fear, students indicated that, ironically, it was engaging in art that helped overcome the fear of art. Bayles and Orland (1993) know that art and fear are dynamically interconnected and it takes courage to engage with the arts:

To make art is to sing with the human voice. To do this you must first learn that the only voice you need is the voice you already have. Artwork is ordinary work, but it takes courage to embrace that work, and wisdom to mediate the interplay of art and fear.

(p. 117)

One of the rewards of confronting and balancing fear of the arts may also provide teachers with a prerequisite skill to overcome their fear of leadership, by using *palpable pedagogy* to "engage in issues that matter" (Bayles & Orland, 1993, p. 17), developing a new vision, drawing on hope, and making a commitment to action for change in the world.

In chapter 7, the final chapter of this study, I will pick up the thread of leadership begun here and discuss the implications of the study for leadership and change more comprehensively. I will also revisit my original review of the literature, examine the limitations of this study, propose future research, and summarize my learning.

Chapter VII: Implications for Leadership and Change

Brief Recapitulation of the Study

This study of the culture and learning generated in my arts-based teacher education course, "Expressive Arts, Leadership, and Change," demonstrated the invigorating potential of the arts, as *palpable pedagogy* to provide educators with a critical pedagogy for social justice education. I employed a reflective ethnographic/autoethnographic research method. As an artist-educator/researcher, involved in teaching a social justice course over the last three summers, I investigated its multiple dimensions and believe that my findings and analysis bulk up the scant, though exceptional, literature in the field exploring the utilization of the arts in social justice teacher education. I believe the dimensions of *palpable pedagogy* revealed and developed through my investigation add a significant contribution, both theoretical and pedagogical, to the field of social justice teacher education.

Literature Review Revisited

In my literature review, I discussed the roots of art, beauty, justice, and humanity via Scarry (1999), Dissanayake (1990, 1992, 2000), and Kenny (1982, 1989, 1998, 2006). I discussed aesthetic education via Greene (1979, 1995, 2007a-h) and Eisner (1991, 2002a, 2008). Critical theory and humanistic education were discussed via Giroux (2006) and Bell and Schneidewind (1987), and their subsequent contributions (Bell, 2003a, 2003b; Schneidewind & Davidson, 2006) were noted. Since then, Bell (in press) has also developed a creative program, called the "Storytelling Project," to help inner-city high school students understand and deal creatively and effectively with issues of race, through stories, storytelling, and artist-facilitated art workshops.

Working in the same vein, but not mentioned in my initial literature review, are Cammarota and Fine (2008), who have contributed to the literature by offering a framework for a critical research methodology known as youth-led participatory action research, or YPAR. Through this process, the researchers involve students in developing their own research questions and problems relevant to them and, using dramatic techniques, students learn how to act upon them.

I discussed multicultural art teacher education, where the bulk of arts-based social justice teacher education is practiced via Noel (2003) and arts-based teacher education via Kenny (1998) and Shapiro (2004, 2006). Of all the educator researchers working in the field, the work of Kenny (1998) in indigenous social justice teacher education, Shapiro (2004, 2006) in educational leader social justice education, and Noel (2003) in art teacher social justice education, represents the nature of the work to which my research is most closely related.

Finally, I discussed social justice adult and community education via Clover and Stalker (2007) and aesthetic leadership via Hansen et al. (2007), and Ladkin (2008). I will proceed with my discussion of the relevance of my study to leadership and change with the insights of these aesthetic leadership authors in the following section.

Relevance of the Study to Leadership and Change

As I consider the relevance of this study to the practice of leadership and change, two streams of thought converge for me. The first stream of thought ties the study to the emerging literature on aesthetic leadership. The second stream of thought ties this study to the literature on teacher leadership development. I will discuss both streams in this section.

Aesthetic Leadership and the Art of Leadership

Hansen et al. (2007) and Ladkin (2008), who I introduced in my literature review, spearheaded the emerging literature on aesthetic leadership and frame the nature of leadership as a relational, embodied activity. Leaving the exploration of the behavioral characteristics of leaders to other leadership theorists, Ladkin instead focuses on "the way in which those behaviors are enacted" (p. 31).

Like Read (1965) and Eisner (2002a, 2008), Ladkin (2008) is a strong proponent of unfettering aesthetic ways of knowing, sensing, and acting in relationship as leader. Ladkin urges leaders to position beauty to assist them in the beautiful alignment of purpose with the ethical (here meaning *for the good*). As we experienced with Kenny's (1998) sense of beauty, Ladkin places great emphasis on congruence, and like Vaill (1989), she sees the relational dimensions of aesthetic leadership much like a performing art. Greene (1995) posits that encounters with the arts "move us to want to restore some kind of order, to repair, to heal" (p. 123). If the relational role of the leader is to provide cohesion and alignment of purpose and action, the nature of aesthetics with its synergistic powers have much to contribute to this endeavor.

For Eisner (2002a), experience in the arts cultivates and embodies somatic knowledge, honors tacit knowing, and generates modes of thinking and feeling that are integrated. "As we learn through the arts," he says, "we become qualitatively intelligent" (p. 6). Further, Eisner says that our somatic processes rely on feeling in much the same way an artist uses sensibilities in the creative process. Both Read (1965) and Eisner (2002a) insist that the aim of education should be the preparation of artists. They are not talking literally about painters, sculptors, or even poets, although I would not discount this prospect. They are referring to "individuals who have developed the ideas, the sensibilities, the skills, and the imagination to create work that is well proportioned, skillfully executed, and imaginative, regardless of the domain in which an individual works" (Eisner, 2002b, p. 13).

Leadership has long been thought of as an art and associated with creativity (Bennis, 1994; Bolman & Deal, 1991; Gardner, 1995; Heifetz, 1994; Senge, 1990; Vaill, 1989). Bolman and Deal (1991) propose that leaders should recognize the importance of poetry and philosophy and "embrace the fundamental values of human life and human spirit" (p. 451). Leaders, in Bolman and Deal's paradigm will "understand the importance of knowing and caring for themselves and those with whom they work. They will, in short, be architects, catalysts, advocates, prophets, and poets" (p. 451).

Senge (1990), too, asks, "How, then, do leaders help people achieve a view of reality, such as the artist's, as a medium for creating rather than as a source of limitation? . . . This is the task of the leader as teacher" (p. 353) and, I would add, the teacher as leader *and* change agent.

Eisner (2002b) sidelines the idea of a revolution in education in favor of "ideas that inspire new visions, values, and especially new practices" (p. 13). Teachers trained in social justice through the arts are more likely to develop the sensibilities, skills, vision, values, and become facile with new practices fueled by the imagination to help initiate and create positive change in education. "Aesthetic qualities are not restricted to the arts," says Eisner, "their presence depends upon how we choose to experience the world" (2002b, p. 231).

Kelly and Leggo (2008), too, imagine change in education in terms of evolution rather than revolution. They see education evolving from the information age to a conceptual age, where ideas are shared communally, not privately owned:

As we move from the Information Age into the Conceptual Age, educational culture must shift to adapt. The predominant educational culture of standardization and convention must give way to a more balanced educational landscape that accommodates and embraces an educational culture of creativity. (prologue)

201

These authors position creativity as a primary rationale for education, and while not speaking specifically to social justice teacher educators, they speak to *all* educators about the importance of imagination and through it the creative exercises and expressions that are enabled.

For Maxcy's (1995) the revolution that is necessary in education is a revolution in *thinking* that involves sensitivity to the aesthetic quality of schools "as spaces laced with a variety of values beyond those of rational and technical sorts" (p. 156). His vision of change in education eloquently characterized in the passage below gives yet another conception of moral, ethical, and flexible spaces for learning:

> If we think of the moral school as an artist's studio, we are able to use pragmatic metaphors to better approximate a revolution in thinking about the organization and function of schools. Take, for example, the school as a weaver's studio in which the artist-educator comes to inquire into and understand competing values—people's desires, needs, and goals—as threads of experience that must be interwoven into a tapestry of meaning. The educator qua artist is able to take the point of view of others with their interests and desires and to seek a harmonious whole-a moral ideal space within which competing interests become harmonious. (p. 169)

DeCantias (1996), an artist-in-residence at the Center for Creative Leadership in Washington, D.C., speaks of the arts in leadership development more literally and her experience reflects my own experience with my students—giving added hope to those who would work toward the leader as artist movement as she shares her positive experiences working with leaders:

> I have been continually delighted and amazed during several years of working with adults in organizations to find that every one of them has a capacity for creating artistically and seeing meaning in their creations that speaks to them about their sense of purpose as leaders. (p. 88)

For Greene (1995), the skills that the arts develop are critical in developing our "social imagination," which she describes as "the capacity to invent visions of what should be and what might be in our deficient society, on the streets were we live, in our schools" (p. 5). As weavers of social imagination for change in schools, teachers are involved in the process of leadership all the time, as they are aligning their values and helping to make meaning and manifest cohesion of purpose aesthetically. Thus, their

202

authentic human, mindful, ethical, and moral way of being is perceived as beautiful.

Ladkin (2008) characterizes this aesthetic way of being a leader as one that is rarely examined, but very much in need of being recognized:

> Leading beautifully speaks to a quality of being—one honed through the development of self-mastery, and quickened through the congruence of one's acts with their "measured" expression. It also alerts us to the possibility of a leader's goals being directed towards the best of human purposes. (p. 40)

As an ally in developing teachers as leaders whose "goals are directed towards the best of human purposes" (Ladkin, 2008, p. 40), arts-based social justice teacher education allows teachers to develop their aesthetic leadership, through the development of their senses, heightened awareness through multiple media/sensory processes, and experiential teaching skills and methods, as transformative pedagogies to which Greene (1995) refers. Through these aesthetic processes and their presence, teachers as leaders can concretely manifest change in schools. Through their experience, understanding, and learning of the kind they experienced in the "Expressive Arts, Leadership, and Change" course, my students have become more attentive to beauty, as well as other aesthetic responses, and, as a result, will value those responses for the "sensory, spiritual, and moral knowledge with which they are invested" (Ladkin, 2008, p. 40). I believe that it is this kind of knowledge that will equip, support, and guide them as teacher-leaders for social justice work in schools.

Leadership Development of Teachers: Reflective Teacher Leaders

Tyack and Cuban (1995) view reflective teachers as the movers and makers of change:

> Better schooling will result in the future as it has in the past and does now chiefly from the steady, reflective efforts of the practitioners who work in schools. . . . In recent years, policy elites have often bypassed teachers and discounted their knowledge of what schools are like today. . . . Teachers do not have a monopoly on educational wisdom, but their first-hand perspectives on schools and their responsibility for carrying out official policies argue for their centrality in school reform efforts. (p. 135)

Like McGhan (2002), I am optimistic about "what teachers can accomplish on their own" (p. 539). In her research, Lattimer (2007) identified time for reflection, dialogue, and essential questioning, as key qualities found in schools where teachers are most likely to develop and grow as leaders. These are the very same pedagogical practices in which my students engaged during their time in the "Expressive Arts, Leadership, and Change" course. As we have seen in this study, the arts gave these key practices holographic dimension by engaging the senses, emotions, and imagination, through tangible media, and by so doing, deepened teachers' experience of these key enabling, leadership-building qualities.

Teachers are ideally positioned as leaders and change agents because they are working at the grass roots of the school experience. Shapiro's (2004) definition of social justice issues in schools provides a clear path to an awareness of the issues that will require the teacher-as-leaders' attention:

Social justice issues in school communities are those problems that involve unfair and unequal power relationships in schools that are expressions of larger oppressions in our society, such as racism, heterosexism, classism, sexism, ableism, and anti-Semitism. These unfair and oppressive power relationships in the school community often result in unearned privilege for some groups of people and loss of power and privilege for others. (p. 208)

Finally, a reminder to teacher-leaders that the social justice work ahead of them is demanding and to gain and sustain, to thrive and not just survive is their mission— the wisdom of the heart and a commitment to collaborate is required. Leadership theorists Heifetz and Linsky (2002) give guidance for a heart-centered approach to leading:

A sacred heart allows you to feel, hear, and diagnose, even in the midst of your mission, so that you can accurately gauge different situations and respond appropriately. Otherwise, you simply cannot accurately assess the impact of the losses you are asking people to sustain, or comprehend the reasons behind their anger. Without keeping your heart open, it becomes difficult, perhaps impossible, to fashion the right response and to succeed or come out whole. (p. 228)

Leading beautifully would require nothing less.

Just as it was for art, the primary antagonist to leadership identified in this study is *fear*. As we have seen, fear can be a significant foe, occluding possibility and short-circuiting the imagination—two very important ingredients needed for social justice leadership. Nelson Mandela (1994), in his inaugural speech as the first democratically elected president of South Africa, emphasized the quandary that fear can create for leaders and predicted that "As we are liberated from our own fear, our presence automatically liberates others." The arts assist us both to imagine ourselves as leaders and be perceived aesthetically as a leader authentically involved in libratory action.

Suggestions for Future Explorations and Research

Although, I feel each of the themes identified through this research are worthy of further study, I would like to pursue further ethnographic inquiry into the phenomenon of fear of the arts in the hopes of gaining a deeper understanding of this phenomenon and to help develop strategies to buffer or entirely ameliorate it effects. I believe that students' participation as co-researchers in this type of study would not only contribute to the field of self-study research, but would provide significant insights into the dynamics of fear of the arts in the field of education. Through their collective participation in this inquiry, teachers can help develop possible solutions for overcoming fear of the arts, so that the arts may work their magic on their students' lives. Additionally, in the context of fear, pre-service teachers' fear of leadership would be a worthy, compelling, and challenging topic to explore to advance the field of teacher-leader development.

In addition to fear, the other identified sub-themes were pleading to be explored in more detail, but, due to the space limitations of the book, this was not possible. However, in a subsequent article, I hope to elaborate more of my findings regarding art-generated compassion and empathy. In addition, the data contain significant insight on the sub-theme of action. Students collaboratively created action plans and presented them experientially to the class, demonstrating creative mastery of the use of the arts for social justice education. I would very much like to write about some of the *palpable pedagogy* my students produced during the course.

Another compelling theme that emerged from these data, like a melody to a song beckoning to be sung, was that of the healing power of the arts. Many artist researchers have written about the healing power of the arts (Allen, 1995; Kenny, 1982, 1989, 2006; McNiff, 1992; Rhyne, 1996; Richards, 1989; Rogers, 1993). As social justice work is motivated by an impulse to heal injustice, I believe the arts can be a valiant ally in this work, as Kenny (1982, 1989, 2006), Noel (2003), and Rogers (1993) have already noted in their research. I would very much like to build upon their pioneering work and explore this sub-theme in more detail at a future time.

Finally, I would like to advance the idea, whose roots may also very well go back to arts' beginnings, that making the arts available to everyone *is* social justice. Hopefully, I will have the opportunity to further develop this revelation and, through my writing, to advocate for the use of the arts globally in education—particularly for students who are egregiously deprived of them for months, and sometimes years, of their school experience.

Challenges of the Study and Findings

The scope of this study was vast, spanning a three-year period and involving 37 graduate students. The arts-based ethnographic/autoethnographic methodology I employed allowed me to mine a very rich and deep lode of contextually-rich lived experience, and amass visually stunning and diverse data—and through them, deep understanding of the complexities and dynamics of the unique arts-based culture that emerged. The benefits of the plethora of data for me, as a researcher, (and, I believe, for you as the reader) are innumerable, some more immediately obvious than others.

Ironically, though, this vast plethora of data also seemed a burden at times. Decisions on what to report about the culture (when every subtle detail seemed too important and fascinating to be left out) were difficult. Equally challenging was how to adequately *write* culture that encompassed so many dimensions of learning and teaching, manifested through multi-dimensional art forms. Data streams seemed to overflow their banks with a bounty of kaleidoscopic insights into the culture and its significance.

Humphreys et al. (2003) characterize ethnography as an exploratory, creative, and interpretive process and compare the ethnographer to a jazz musician. This metaphor speaks to my experience most eloquently because, embedded in the metaphor, is the dynamic I felt as a researcher. My experience of the dynamic was the challenge of alternation from my solo, or my individual, to ensemble, or my collective, functions. As an artist-researcher/educator it was challenging, at times, for me to strike a balance between myself and others. Examining my own process as college professor teaching social justice teacher education through the arts and dynamically changing as a person in the process sometimes was simultaneously (and sometimes in alternation with my focus on my students' learning processes) challenging. My role in that process and our co-creation of the culture was a challenge, a balancing act, and ultimately, richly rewarding. Choosing how to contribute to, and later, how to represent such a rich learning culture, while staying connected to my personal and professional growth and learning required flexibility, multiple perspective-taking, and creative improvisation on my part—so, in very many ways, similar to a Jazz musician.

206

Closing

In this study, I have articulated how beauty, justice, and truth are joined in social justice teacher education through the arts. I have described how the arts, joining the body (senses), heart (emotions), and mind (imagination), meshing each to the other, resulted in *palpable pedagogy* for social justice education. I want to assure the reader that my intention has been, by no means, to trivialize the arts, but, on the contrary, to expand the understanding of their effects and influence and to draw on their deep roots and re-conceptualize the role of the arts in teacher education for social justice. Dissanayake (1992) supports such a re-conceptualization and, going one step farther, conceives of the arts as a naturally human disposition and, like Kenny (2000), advocates for their recognition and reintegration in human life:

> Art is a normal and necessary behavior of human beings that, like other common and universal human occupations and preoccupations such as talking, working, exercising, playing, socializing, learning, loving, and caring, should be recognized, encouraged, and developed in everyone. (p. 225)

It is my sincere hope that the results of the study I have presented and interpreted will contribute to the emerging scholarship and research in the field of arts-based social justice teacher education and has evoked the aesthetic awe and enrichment that I, myself, experienced repeatedly while teaching "Expressive Arts, Leadership, and Change." It has been my privilege to share the results of my study and new understanding and appreciation of this unique culture of the arts in social justice education and what it has to teach. Through their courage, my students have taught me the most profound lesson of all. The fear of art, the fear of leadership, and the fear of change can be overcome, which is what makes social justice teacher education, in the final analysis, an aesthetic imperative.

APPENDICES

Appendix A

SYLLABUS (Composite 2006-2008)

I. Instructor

Lucy Barbera

Humanistic Multicultural Education Program

Office hours by appointment

Phone: 845-417-4558

Email: Barberal@newpaltz.edu

II. Description

The expressive arts can be utilized in identifying issues of injustice and envisioning and leading change initiatives that address social justice issues in schools and community organizations. This reflective and experiential course will explore practical, arts-based teaching and learning strategies.

Course Description

The expressive arts can be applied in identifying and envisioning and leading change initiatives that address social justice issues in schools and community organizations. This reflective and experiential course will explore practical, arts-based teaching and learning strategies that provide students with methods for leading change through engagement, critical thought, and action through the arts. The course will support students in developing and leading creative and equitable change initiatives in schools, human service agencies, and community settings. Through a focus on theory, practice, and reflection, students will learn that the expressive arts can be clearly and consciously applied to foster positive change in institutions and society. Students will gain the theoretical and practical skills needed to put appropriate methods into action in their professional work, as well as the skills to lead these initiatives

III. Course Objectives

1.Expressive Arts Methods: To learn expressive arts methods as tools for engagement in and exploration of social justice issues. This includes the visual and performing arts.

2.Gain Understanding and Develop Repertoire of Skills: To gain an understanding of the connections between the arts, education and social justice. Increase students' repertoire of creative arts processes that support and foster change, using arts-based strategies to facilitate engagement with social justice issues.

3. Leader as Learner: To gain understanding of and skills in leading that are related to learning to act effectively in the real time of situations which are constructed contextually rather than leadership as dictated by a "how to" theory.

4.Theory and Application: To gain knowledge of the theoretical, historical, and practical legacy demonstrating the vital role the expressive arts have played in creating positive change in human history and more recently in education and human service settings.

5.Practice of Methods in Action: To facilitate the creation of an action plan that utilizes the expressive arts to teach social justice. Practice in how to foster positive change in each student's particular work situation so that their students in turn may do the same. Practice and adapt skills gained to particular education and/or human service settings.

IV. Course Topics

This course focuses on establishing a model for the Expressive Arts as a potent vehicle for leading positive change. The emphasis will be on expanding the learner's understanding of the connections between the arts, education and social justice. By increasing their repertoire of strategies that encourage engagement in and exploration of social justice issues through the arts, students will learn how to engage others in Expressive Arts processes that allow for reflection, exploration of self-identity in relation to social justice, raise awareness through dialogue, and facilitate the opportunity to create change in community. Students will engage in intensive work experiencing the Expressive Arts methods and their utilization for leading change in the Educational and Human Service setting.

V. Specific Topics to Be Covered`

1. Introduction

Introductions, overview of course and expectations. Review syllabus and bibliography. Introduce the Lincoln Center Institute Capacities for Teaching and Learning at the Samuel Dorskey Museum of Art. Choose artwork that can be seen as autobiographical. Journal. Dyad/Triad/Large Group Process.

2. Honoring the Learning Community and Individual Identity through Art Making and Dialogue

Honoring the learning community through mutual support and experiencing the methods that foster trust, openness, and honesty will be facilitated through dyad, triad and large group work. The classroom community includes a wide range of people with varied personal gifts and professional expertise, enriching the opportunities for students to learn from one another.

Expressive arts methods demonstrated through personal story/poetry creation: "I Am From" and/or multi-modal Educational Autobiography.

Essential Question: What are expressive arts and how might they be used for social justice work?

Assigned Readings:

Dissanayake, E. (1992). *Homo aestheticus, Where art comes from and why,* Chapter 1

Marshall, C. and Oliva, M. (2006) *Leadership for social justice,* Chapter 1-2

Ganim, B. & Fox, S. (1999). *Visual journaling: Going deeper than words,* Chapter 1

Palmer, P. (1998). *The Courage to teach.* Chapter 1.

The Expressive Arts Methods: Integration of movement, art, sound, music, writing and guided imagery to build repertoire of expressive arts methods for social justice work. Each session will include discussion of application and adaptation to student's professional work situation.

*Essential Questions: What is social justice? How does my context (class, race, ethnicity, gender, sexual orientation) impact how I go about the work of change? What are the implications of our locations and the locations of the communities in which we

211

work re: making change? How might art/expressive arts help foster social justice in our schools, communities and larger world?

Assigned Readings:

Marshall, C. and Oliva, M. (2006) Leadership for Social Justice, Chapter 3-4

DeCiantis, C. (1996) What does drawing my hand have to do with leadership? A look at

the process of leaders becoming artists. *Journal of Aesthetic Education*, 30(4), 87-97

Ganim, B. & Fox, S. (1999). *Visual journaling: Going deeper than words*, Chapter 2

Palmer, P. (1998). The Courage to teach. Chapter 2.

3. Cultural Plunge/Cross Cultural Interview: Students participate in cultural plunge (Ryan and Katz, 2006) report out on related homework assignments throughout the course. Dialogue and report out on: common themes, learning, application.

Working with Groups, Developing Community Modeling of Professional Application: Invited guest, who is working for social justice, using the arts in the field of education and/or human services, will facilitate the use of Expressive Arts experientially demonstrating application in real world settings and will present example of her/his work followed by discussion re: application in student's field of focus.

Essential Questions:

Questions will be collectively developed by students and the invited guest.

Inquiry Questions and Contexts for Social Justice Work – Guest Artist- Elise Gold, MSW Facilitates Playback Theater in Schools to explore dimensions of "isms" **or**

Guest Artist – Susan Togut, MFA Facilitates Demonstrates Public Art Projects that foster Social Justice

Exploration through expressive arts of inquiry questions centered on social justice themes (classism, racism, sexism, ableism, heterosexism, anti-Semitism, ageism, etc.) as they are manifested in policies, places and people in schools/human service settings.

*Essential Questions:

What are aesthetic models of leadership and change and how do they differ from other models? How are current methods of change different from and complementary to aesthetic models? To whom does "art" belong? Who has access to the arts? Who does not? Why?

Listening, Communication, and Reflection

The person centered approach will be modeled throughout the course. Theory and discussion of person centered philosophy and facilitation will be based on readings and observation of our own processes, through reflection, dialogue, and in community.

Practice communication and listening skills working in triads. Three roles will be experienced on a rotational basis. Examination of processes, roles, feedback, questions and answers regarding

the use of the expressive arts to build listening and communication skills to support social justice inquiry and change. Time for Reflection will be scheduled into each session via journaling and/or art making.

Film Viewing and Dialogue: View The Letter: The Somali Invasion of Lewiston Maine. Create artwork in response to the film. Process film and share artwork in Dialogue Group.

Essential Questions:

What questions do we ask when we encounter social injustice? How can we learn to listen in a new way? What are the "deep structures" that prevent dialogue on social justice issues in schools and human service organizations?

Assigned readings:

Marshall, C. and Oliva, M. (2006) *Leadership for Social Justice*, Chapter 7-8

Greene, M. (1995). *Releasing the imagination: Essays on education, the arts, and social*
Change. Jigsaw, each dialogue group select one chapter each.
Palmer, P. (1998). The Courage to teach. Chapter 3.

A Movement Model for Social Change and Leading Change

Using Parker Palmer's "Movement Model for Social Change" as a framework for positioning ourselves on the continuum and developing strategies to lead change. Examples of grass-roots activism by ourselves and historical leaders will be identified and analyzed using Palmer's model. Examine the writings of effective change leaders in history. Identify commonalities and unique aspect of these leaders including their philosophies. Dialogue and process in Dialogue Groups.

Essential Questions:

How can teachers and human service providers lead change? How can students and clients lead change?

Assigned Readings:

Marshall, C. and Oliva, M. (2006) Leadership for Social Justice, Chapter 9-10

Ganim, B. & Fox, S. (1999). *Visual journaling: Going deeper than words*, Chapter 3

Ongoing Coaching and Understanding the Power of Expressive Arts for Social Change Using a coaching model, students will bring issues (case studies) for collective problem solving, guidance, and inspiration. Practice strategies in the field and report back on results. Additionally, students will explore, through readings and review of experiential work, the historical and current practical applications of the Expressive Arts and their power to facilitate social change.

Classroom Explorations:

Mask Making-*Masks of Power* exploring issues of power and prejudice that create *isms* visually through mask making.

Art and Fear: Visual, Textual, and Dramatic investigation of the fear of art.

Essential Questions:

How do educational institutions replicate and perpetuate the existing power imbalances of the dominant culture?

In what ways do educational institutions set up art as a privilege rather than a human right?

What interventions can be facilitated for change to occur on personal, school community, and policy level?

Assigned Readings:

Dissanayake, E. (1992). *Homo aestheticus, Where art comes from and why.* Chapter 2-4

Marshall, C. and Oliva, M. (2006) *Leadership for social justice*, Chapter 11-12

Greene, M. (1995). Art and imagination: Reclaiming the sense of possibility. *Phi Delta Kappan*, 76(5), 378-382.

Palmer, P. (1998). The Courage to teach. Chapter 4.

4. Action Plan for Integration of Ex. Arts in Professional Setting

Students form cooperative teams (four students) to begin process of developing of action plan using expressive arts to raise consciousness or create change re: social justice issues. Students will cluster around common topics of interest, target population, methods, application and approach. Use the Theater of the Oppressed (Parade of Images) to explore personal vision for social justice in your world.

Essential Questions:

*Whose interests are served? Whose interests are not served? Who decides? What assumptions are we making about students, clients, and/or families? Who is silenced? Silent? Why? How might we individually and collectively create a just classroom, school, agency? Why?

Assigned Readings:

Marshall, C. and Oliva, M. (2006) Leadership for Social Justice, Chapter 13-14

Clover, C. & Stalker, J. *The Arts and Social Justice: Re-crafting Adult Education and Community Cultural Leadership.* Student selected chapters.

Classroom Explorations:

Masks –Polarities Creating masks as a way to reflect and discover our individual and collective power to make change from the bottom up.

Exploration of polarities of social justice issue utilizing inside and outside of the mask.

*Essential Questions:

What is power? What is courage? What kind of power do you have? What kind of power do others have to make change and what are the sources of this power? What is the difference between power with and power over?

Assigned Readings:

Marshall, C. and Oliva, M. (2006) *Leadership for social justice*, Chapter 15

Jones, A T. (1992). Mask making: The use of the expressive arts in leadership development. *Journal of Experiential Education*, 15(1), 28-34.

Assigned Readings:

Ganim, B. & Fox, S. (1999). *Visual journaling: Going deeper than words*, Chapter 5

Spehler, M.R., & Slattery, P. (1999). Voices of imagination: The artist as prophet in the process of social change. *International Journal of Leadership in Education*, 2(1), 1-12.
Professional Action Plan Collaboratively Developed: Design presentation, include how to implement in the field, collaborating with team members. Students will be given time to dialogue with group, work with their team, report field progress, refine and re-draft final action plans.:

Essential Questions:

How is trust fostered? How does one create the conditions for openness and honesty within groups for building community? How do these actions for exploring and creating social justice?

Assigned Readings:

Dissanayake, E. (1992). *Homo aestheticus, Where art comes from and why*. Chapters 5-7

Stuhr, P. L. (1994) Multicultural art education and social reconstruction. *Studies in Art Education*, 35(3),171-178
Unnseld, T. S. (1996). Cultures unmasked. School Arts, 95(6), 28.

5. Students Leading Change – Part I

Presentation of Action Plan for Application: Using experiential facilitation methods, students, in teams, will present their action plan by demonstrating a

professional application of the Expressive Arts to foster social justice and change. Group feedback will target strengths of the plan and areas for expansion or modification.

Assigned Readings:

Dissanayake, E. (1992). *Homo aestheticus, Where art comes from and why*, Chapters8-10.

6. Cont'd. Presentation of Action Plans for Application: Students Leading Change

Feedback, networking and planning for future collaboration in the Expressive Arts and social justice work. The closing session will be used to summarize the work of the course in utilizing creative processes. Students will complete course evaluation

Final Exam,_Self-Learning and Evaluation and Synthesis Paper: Due by Last Day of Class.

* Essential Questions: (L. Shapiro, 2004; Barbera, 2009)

VI. Course Assignments/Requirements:

a. Requirement I.

Readings: Readings including Required Text and Additional Required Readings are listed as a. Assigned Readings are due for the next class (ex. reading listed under class 1 are due for class 2). Selected chapters and articles listed, but not found in required texts, will be available for loan and duplication. Some additional articles may be assigned. Students are expected to complete all reading assignments. *(inquiry and intellectual growth)*

Required Readings:

Clover, C. & Stalker, J. *The Arts and Social Justice: Re-crafting Adult Education and Community Cultural Leadership.* London: NIACE.

Dissanayake, E. (1992). *Homo aestheticus, Where art comes from and why.* Seattle: University of Washington Press.

Marshall, C. and Oliva, M. (2006). *Leadership for social justice: Making revolutions in education.* Boston: Pearson Education, Inc.

Ganim, B. & Fox, S. (1999). *Visual journaling: Going deeper than words.* Wheaton: The Theosophical Publishing House

Palmer, P. (1998). *The Courage to teach.* San Francisco: Jossey-Bass.

Please note:

Additional Leadership Articles will be assigned.

Additional Readings on Electronic reserve: DeCiantis (1996), Greene (1995),

217

Jones (1992), Spehler & Slattery (1999), Unseld (1996).

Expressive Arts Toolkit (Available at Mannys in New Paltz)

Process Journal: Students will be required to maintain a <u>process journal</u>, which will include:

- a weekly **response/reaction** to ideas, readings, and class experience for possible application of methods for future use.
- **case studies** for collective problem solving, guidance, and inspiration will be documented including practiced strategies in the field and reports back on results.
- **action plan notes** documenting action plan development. *(professionalism and advocacy for students)*

Ongoing Development of Action Plan: The development of an <u>action plan</u> utilizing the expressive arts to teach social justice and lead positive change in each student's particular work situation. Action plans will be cooperatively developed, redeveloped and refined on an ongoing basis. Action Plan will specify what issues will be addressed in the student's professional setting including where, when, and how implementation will take place. *(appreciation of human diversity)*

Final Action Plan/Presentation: Student will cooperatively design an action plan, utilizing the expressive arts for fostering/teaching social justice within the context of their professional work setting, submit written version of the plan and experientially facilitate the class to demonstrate the cogent action plan. Action plans will include a description of the

- setting of plan,
- group with whom issues will be addressed,
- social justice issues that will be addressed
- expressive arts processes used to explore social justice issues
- final processing strategies and next steps. *(democratic citizenship)*

218

a. Requirement II.

Synthesis Paper (6-8 pgs.) Theory and application will be synthesized based on course texts, classroom experiences, and action plan development. Students will write analytical paper demonstrating their understandings of how to use/take leadership in utilizing the expressive arts for the exploration of social justice issues in education and human service settings. *(inquiry, intellectual growth, professionalism, appreciation of human diversity)*

Self-Learning and Evaluation Paper (5-7 pgs.). Using the course objectives as a frame, students will recapitulate their learning process, chronicling both formative knowledge gained and skills learned. Students will summarize and evaluate their learnings, personal and professional relevance of skills and learning, and feasibility of future professional application. *(inquiry, intellectual growth, professionalism, appreciation of human diversity, advocacy for students, and democratic citizenship)*

Final Exam Students will be given a social justice issue in the form of a case study and asked to propose possible solutions utilizing the arts to explore and foster positive social change. Students will describe theoretical framework for their solutions. *(professionalism, democratic citizenship, appreciation of human diversity, advocacy for students)*

b. Rubric for Grading/Assessing Each Course Requirement

- Participation – Attendance 10%
- Journal entry of Expressive Arts Journal. (Addressing readings, class experience, case study) AND
- Journal entry of Action Plan Notes (addressing application of methods in professional setting) 10%
- Final Action Plan (First draft due mid-way through course, before your scheduled presentation) and Presentation 25%
- Synthesis Paper, 6-8 pages 25%

- Self Learning and Evaluation Paper, 5-7 pages 15%
- Final Exam 15%

My Expectations:

- To begin and end class on time
- To receive assignments when they are due. Late assignments will be accepted only if previous arrangements have been made.
- To give no incompletes for the course unless explicitly negotiated in advance. Otherwise, grades will be based on assignments completed.
- To have people take advantage of my consultation if you need help with the material. Please feel free to set up an appointment with me at a mutually agreeable time.
- To receive work of graduate quality.

Criteria for Evaluation Written Work:

- Thoroughness of discussion: Take the time to explore the many facets of an issue; give adequate expression to your ideas and provide examples to support your points.
- Depth of understanding material: Demonstrate the ability to analyze, synthesize and apply material both intellectually and personally.
- Clarity of expression: Use language and vocabulary that are alive with our own voice and that convey directly and effectively what you think and feel.
- General manner of presentation: Carefully organize and proofread, check spelling, grammar and punctuation, use nonsexist language.
- Meeting the objectives of the assignment: Your work should reflect the purpose of the assignment and answer the questions posed.

If resources to improve writing are needed they are available at:

The Writer's Assistance Program, Humanities B2, 257-3591.

New York State Learning Standards Addressed:

- **The Arts:** Standard 1: Creating, Performing, and Participating in the Arts

    Standard 2: Knowing and Using Arts Materials and Resources

220

Standard 3:   Responding to and Analyzing Works of Art

Standard 4:   Understanding the Cultural Contributions of the Arts

- **English Language Arts:**

    Standard 2:   Language for Literary Response and Expression

    Standard 3:   Language for Critical Analysis and Evaluation

    Standard 4:   Language for Social Interaction

- **Career Development and Occupational Studies:**

    Standard 2:   Integrated Learning

VII. Bibliography

A. Contemporary References

Adams, M., Bell, L.A., & Griffin, P. (Eds.). (2007). *Teaching for diversity and social justice: a sourcebook*. New York, NY: Routledge.

Allen, P.B. (1995). *Art as a way of knowing: A Guide to self-knowledge and spiritual fulfillment through creativity*. Boston: Shambhala.

Barone, T. (2000). *Aesthetics, politics, and educational inquiry: Essays and examples*. New York: Peter Lang Publishing

Booth, E. (1997). *The everyday work of art: How artistic experience can transform your life*. Sourcebooks.

Burnham, L.F., & Durland, S. (1998). *The citizen artist: Twenty years of art in the public arena* (First ed. Vol. 1). New York: Critical Press.

Christensen, L. (2000). *Reading, writing and rising up: Teaching about social justice and the power of the written word*. Milwaukee: Rethinking Schools.

DeCiantis, C. (1996) What does drawing my hand have to do with leadership? A look at the process of leaders becoming artists. *Journal of Aesthetic Education*, 30(4), 87-97.

221

Delacruz, E. M. (1995). Multiculturalism and art education: Myths, misconceptions, mis-directions. *Art Education*, 48(3), 57-61.

Diehn, G. (2002). *The Decorated page: Journals, scrapbook, and albums made simply beautiful*: Sterling Publisher.

Dissanayake, E. (1992). *Homo aestheticus, Where art comes from and why.* Seattle: University of Washington Press.

Eisner, E. (2002). *The arts and the creation of mind.* New Haven: Yale University Press.

Felshin, N.(1995). *But is it art? The spirit of art as activism.* Seattle: Bay Press.

Ganim, B. & Fox, S. (1999). *Visual journaling: Going deeper than words.* Wheaton: The Theosophical Publishing House.

Gardiner, M., Enomoto, E., & Grogan, M. (Eds.) (2000). *Coloring outside the lines: Mentoring women into school leadership.* Albany: State University of New York Press.

Giroux, H. (1997) *Pedagogy and the politics of hope: Theory, culture, and schooling.* Boulder: Westview.

Glickman, C. (Ed.). (2004). Letters to the next President: what we can do about *the real Crisis in Public Education.* New York: Teachers College Press

Greene, M. (1995). Art and imagination: Reclaiming the sense of possibility. *Phi Delta Kappan*, 76(5), 378-382.

Greene, M. (1995). *Releasing the imagination: Essays on education, the arts, and social change.* San Francisco: Jossey-Bass.

Irvine, J. J. (Ed.). (1997). *Critical knowledge for diverse teachers and learners.*
222

Washington D.C.: The American Association of Colleges for Teacher Education.

Larson, C., & Ovando, C. (2001). *The color of bureaucracy: The politics of equity in multicultural school communities.* New York: Wadsworth.

Lee, E., Menkart, D., & Okazawa- Rey, M. (Eds.). (1998). *Beyond heroes and holidays: A practical guide to K-12 anti- racist, multicultural education and staff development.* Washington D.C.: Network of Educators on the Americas.

Marshall, C. & Oliva, M. (Eds.). (2006). Leadership for social justice: Making revolutions in education. Boston:MA: Pearson Education, Inc.

Mullin, A. (2000). Art, Understanding, and Political Change. Hypatia, 15 3, pgs. 113-201.

Paulus, C. & Horth, D. (1996). Leading Creatively: The Art of making Sense. Journal of Aesthetic Education 30, 4, Pgs. 53-67.

Richards, D. (1995). *Artful work: Awakening joy, meaning, and commitment in the workplace.* San Francisco, CA: Berrett-Koehler Publishers.

Richards, M.C. (1996). *Opening our moral eye: Essays, talks, & poems embracing creativity & community.* Hudson, NY: Lindisfarne Press.

Sapon- Shevin, M. (1999). *Because we can change the world: A practical guide to building cooperative, inclusive classroom communities.* Boston: Allyn and Bacon.

Schniedewind, N. & Davidson, E. (2007). Open minds to equality: A sourcebook of learning activities to affirm diversity and promote equity. Williston:VT: Rethinking Schools.

Sleeter, C., & Grant, C. A. (1999). *Making choices for multicultural education* (Third ed.). Upper Saddle River: Prentice-Hall.

223

Spehler, M.R., & Slattery, P. (1999). Voices of imagination: The artist as prophet in the process of social change. *International Journal of Leadership in Education*, 2(1), 1-12.

Thousand, J.S., Villa, R.A. & Nevin, A.I.(2002). *Creativity & collaborative learning: A practical guide to empowering students, teachers, and families*. Baltimore, MD: Paul H. Brookes Publishing Company.

Unnseld, T. S. (1996). Cultures unmasked. School Arts, 95(6), 28.

B. Traditional References

Barone, T. (1993). Breaking the mold: The new American student as strong poet. *Theory into Practice*, 32(4), 236-243.

Bayles, D. & Orland, T. (1993). *Art and fear: Observations on the perils (and rewards) of artmaking*. Santa Barbara: Capra Press.

Boal, Augusto (1979). *Theatre of the oppressed*. New York, N.Y.: Theatre Communications Group

Dart, D. S. (1982, October). Expressing emotions through masks. *School Arts*, 82(2), 30-32.

Deal, T. E. & Peterson, K.D. (1994). *The leadership paradox: Balancing logic and artistry in schools*. San Francisco: Jossey-Bass.

Hooks, b. (1994). *Teaching to transgress*. New York: Routledge.

Jones, A T. (1992). Mask making: The use of the expressive arts in leadership development. *Journal of Experiential Education*, 15(1), 28-34.

Murray, W. (1994) Face to face with feelings: maskmaking activities for teaching Language, literature and self expression. *Instructor Magazine*,

Raven, Arlene (Ed.) (1993). *Art in the public interest*. New York, N.Y.: DaCapo Press.

Rogers, N. (1993). *The creative connection: Expressive arts as healing*. Palo Alto: Science and Behavior Books.

Segy, L (1976). Modern mask, ancient art. *School Arts*, 92(2), 2S26.

Sivin, C. (1986) *Maskmaking*. Worcester, MA:Davis.

Stuhr, P. L. (1994) Multicultural art education and social reconstruction. *Studies in Art Education*, 35(3),171-178

Appendix B

Lucy Barbera
Study of Classroom Culture in Arts-based
Social Justice Teacher Education
2007
Interview Questions

Introduction to the Interview:

I am interested understanding in the classroom culture as it is experienced by stuents participating in the Expressive Arts, Leadership, and Change course. I am hoping through the interviews I am conducting to identify the essential elements of the learning community's culture from a student's perspective. I have a list of questions but if you find the questions limiting, please let me know and you can simply discuss your experience and tell me about anything that seems important to you to relate regarding the elements of the culture of the learning community.

Did you experience the evolution of what might be described as "a classroom culture" over the duration of this course?

Could you identify the unique elements of the classroom culture in Expressive Arts, Leadership, and Change that set it apart from other courses you have taken in your graduate school experience?

How did these elements enhance or detract from your learning experience?

What, if anything, about the classroom culture, moved you closer to understanding more about yourself personally in relation to social justice?

What about the classroom culture, if anything, moved you closer to understanding more about yourself professionally in relationship to social justice?

Is there a metaphor that that comes to mind when you reflect back on the classroom culture?

Is there an experience that you would be willing to share that illuminates an aspect of the classroom culture as you experienced it in Expressive Arts, Leadership, and Change?

Is there anything else you can share with me to help me understand your experience in this class?

226

Appendix C

I am from....

The Jewish religion and rabbis who taught us ethics

Sunday morning rides with Dad to the Jewish deli across town to by smoked

Whitefish and lox

And sometimes Nova Scotia

Good schools and high expectations

Sunday school at the Reform temple

Potato latkes and Chanukah gelt

Bar Mitzvahs and the relatives in Boston

Cigar-smoking uncles in Jersey

G'zei G'zunt!

a mother who was often angry

who wanted me to be everything she couldn't

a Father who hid his Jewishness to "get ahead"

who spoke Yiddish at home, but was Mr. Brown in public

who was never able to solve that contradiction

parents who "assimilated"

...the Sixties, civil rights marches

and anti-war demonstrations

the University of Chicago

social activism

And then retreat from that activism

personal rebellion

choosing an adult life that was "different"

marrying a man from Wilkes Barre mining country

a machinist

working for Civil Service

and getting by...

...the world of second chances

raising a wonderful son

returning to family

knowing myself the contradictory world of Jewish assimilation

forgiving my parents their intrusions

227

being a good counselor

loving my friends

living in the country, but still attending Shul.

(C.C. 7-7-07)

I Am From

I am from the womb of a diverse Legacy.

I am from sleepless nights in Brooklyn, where you're lucky if the street light was your only light.

I am from the last of the penny candy store generation.

I am from the free summer school lunches and monkey bars.

I am from a young mother and father, learning from me as I learned from them.

I am from where the ice cream song and the police sirens sound the same.

I am from where hope is a whisper from my mother's sweet voice.

I am from an only child's dreams that grew like weeds in the backyard.

I am from public school being the best education around.

I am from the struggle, the trails, and the tribulations.

I am from the Head of Slavery.

I am from the torso of the black Renaissance.

I am the legs of the black power movement.

I am from the feet of the women's Liberation.

I am from the Heart of Justice.

I am from the mind of Change.

I am from a world where the social revolution is soon to come.

I am from you what you are from me. (M.B ., July, 2006)

Teaching and Learning at Lincoln Center Institute ©Lincoln Center Institute 2005, Draft, 7/4/2005.

Lincoln Center|institute
for the arts in education

Teaching and Learning
at Lincoln Center Institute

The Philosophical Foundation

Maxine Greene, Lincoln Center Institute's Philosopher-in-Residence, describes aesthetic education as "...the intentional undertaking designed to nurture appreciative, reflective, cultural, participatory engagements with the arts by enabling learners to notice what there is to be noticed, and to lend works of art their lives in such a way that they can achieve them as variously meaningful." Greene proposes that "When this happens, new connections are made in experience: new patterns are formed, new vistas are opened." [1] Her philosophy posits that understanding a work of art takes place in the continuous interaction between the viewer and the artwork, and neither in the work itself nor solely in the perceiver. Not only does she characterize a work of art as an "inexhaustible resource" for learning; she also proposes that as the perceiver's life changes, so do his/her perceptions of that work. In Greene's words, an interaction with a work of art involves nothing less than "lending it your life."

the Capacities of Aesthetic Learning are:

Deep Noticing
to identify "and articulate layers of detail in a work of art through continuous interaction with it over time.

Embodying
to experience a work of art through your senses, as well as emotionally, and also to physically represent that experience

Questioning
to ask questions throughout your explorations that further your own learning; to ask the question, "What if?"

Identifying Patterns
to group the details you notice, and to see patterns

Making Connections
to connect what you notice and the patterns you see to your prior knowledge and experiences, as well as to others' knowledge and experiences including text and multimedia resources

Exhibiting Empathy
to respect the diverse perspectives of others in our community; to understand the experiences of others emotionally, as well as in thought

Appendix E

GUIDELINES FOR THE DORSKY MUSEUM OF ART SESSION

Expressive Arts, Leadership, and Change

SUNY, New Paltz

Lucy Barbera

July 6, 2007

Step One: Take in the space, the galleries, and the artwork. There will be no formal tour of the Museum. Please take your own tour, at your own personal pace.

Step Two: After you have toured the museum and taken in as much as you feel you can or would like to, select a piece of artwork that interests you, speaks to you, or you find particularly compelling in some way:

What do you **NOTICE*** about this work of art?

-What are the details that resonate with you?

-Does it repulse you?

-Are you able to **EMPATHIZE*** with the emotional perspective that is represented?

-What shapes, colors/or lack of, textures, arrangements, forms, relationships, and **PATTERNS*** interest you?

-Why do they interest you?

- Focusing on one or all of these elements, write about how it/they relate to you, bring up a memory, provoke you to do something you have not done or only do rarely.

Ask QUESTIONS*, i.e:

Why does the cylindrical shape make me feel sad?

Is this work of art choosing me or am I choosing it?

What if I were the artist?

Would I have done something different?

EMBODY* or experience the work of art through your senses and notice any emotion that comes up for you.

MAKE CONNECTIONS* between what you notice and your prior knowledge and experience.

Step Three: Finally, take a few moments to imagine the piece you selected as a self-portrait or autobiography. Take some time to do some reflective writing describing how and why this particular piece says something about you and/or your life journey. Allow this to be a "free writing" - don't worry about spelling, grammar or sentence structure, just allow your thoughts to flow freely. You will not be required to share anything you have written. That will be your choice alone to make.

* Lincoln Center Institute for Teaching and Learning, Capacities of Aesthetic Learning (2005)

References

Adams, M., Bell, L. A., & Griffin, P. (Eds.). (2007). *Teaching for diversity and social justice: A sourcebook*. New York: Routledge.

Albergato-Muterspaw, F., & Fenwick, T. (2007) Passion and politics through song: Recalling music to the arts-based debates in adult education. In D. E. Clover & J. Stalker (Eds.), *The arts and social justice: Re-crafting adult education and community cultural leadership* (pp. 147-164). Gosport, UK: Ashford Colour Press.

Allen, P. (1995). *Art is a way of knowing: A guide to self-knowledge and spiritual fulfillment through creativity*. Boston: Shambhala.

Andreas-Salome, L. (2003). *You alone are real to me: Remembering Rainer Maria Rilke* (A. Von der Lippe, Trans.). Rochester, NY: Steven Huff.

Atkinson, P. (2005). Qualitative research: Unity and diversity. *Forum: Qualitative Social Research, 6*(3). Retrieved February 3, 2009, from http://www.qualitative-research.net/fqs-texte/3-05/05-3-26-e.htm

Ayers, W., & Miller, J. (Eds.). (1998). *A light in dark times: Maxine Greene and the unfinished conversation*. New York: Teachers College Press.

Barbera, L. (2006a). *Autoethnographic journal*. Unpublished.

Barbera, L. (2006b). *Independent learning project*. Unpublished.

Barbera, L. (2006c). *Teaching journal*. Unpublished.

Barbera, L. (2007a). *Independent learning project*. Unpublished.

Barbera, L. (2007b). *Teaching journal*. Unpublished.

Barone, T., & Eisner, E. (1997). Arts-based educational research. In R. M. Jaeger & T. Barone (Eds.), *Complementary methods for research in education* (pp. 73-99). Washington, DC: American Educational Research Association.

Bayles, D., & Orland, T. (1993). *Art and fear: Observations on the perils and rewards of art-making*. Santa Cruz, CA: Image Continuum Press.

Bell. L. (in press). *Storytelling for social justice: Connecting narrative and the arts in antiracist teaching*. New York: Routledge.

Bell, L. A. (2003a). Sincere fictions: The pedagogical challenges of preparing White teachers for multicultural classrooms. *Equity & Excellence in Education, 35*(3), 236-244.

Bell, L. A. (2003b). Telling tales: What stories can teach us about racism. *Race, Ethnicity and Education, 6*(1), 3-28.

232

Bell, L., & Schneidewind, N. (1987). Reflective minds/intentional hearts: Joining humanistic education and critical theory for liberating education. *Journal of Education, 169*(2), 55-77.

Bennis, W. (1994). *On becoming a leader.* Reading, MA: Perseus Books.

Bentz, V., & Shapiro, J. (1998). *Mindful inquiry in social research.* Thousand Oaks, CA: Sage.

Boal, A. (1979). *Theatre of the oppressed.* New York: Theatre Communications Group.

Boje, D. (2001). *Narrative methods for organizational & communication research.* Thousand Oaks, CA: Sage.

Bolman, L., & Deal, T. (1991). *Reframing organizations: Artistry, choice, and leadership.* San Francisco: Jossey-Bass.

Bottoms, G. (2007). *The colorful apocalypse: Journeys in outsider art.* Chicago: University Press.

Brodskaya, N. D. (2007). *Naïve art: Art of century.* New York: Parkstone Press.

Brown, K. M. (2006). Leadership for social justice and equity: Evaluating a transformative framework and andragogy. *Educational Administration Quarterly, 42*(5), 700-745.

Bullough, R.V., Jr., & Baughman, K. (1997). *"First year teacher" eight years later: An inquiry into teacher development.* New York: Teachers College Press.

Bullough, R.V., Jr., & Pinnegar, S. (2001). Guidelines for quality in autobiographical forms of self-study research. *Educational Researcher, 30*(3), 13-21.

Butler, R. (1997). Stories and experiments in social inquiry. *Organization Studies, 18*(6), 927-948.

Cammarota, J., & Fine, M. (2008). Revolutionizing education: Youth participatory action *research in motion.* New York: Routledge.

Charmaz, K. (2005). Grounded theory in the 21st century: Applications for advancing social justice studies. In N. Denzin & Y. Lincoln (Eds.), *The SAGE handbook of qualitative research* (3rd ed.) (pp. 507-534). Thousand Oaks: Sage.

Childs-Bowen, D., & Moller, G. (2000). Principals: Leaders of leaders. *NASSP Bulletin, 84*(616), 27.

Christensen, L. (2000). *Reading, writing, and rising up: Teaching about social justice and the power of the written word.* Milwaukee, WI: Rethinking Schools.

233

Ciuffetelli-Parker, D., Fazio, X., Volante, L., & Cherubini, L. (2008). Relationship matters: Negotiating and maintaining partnerships in a unique teacher education program. *Action in Teacher Education, 30*(3), 39-53.

Clark, C. (2005). Diversity initiatives in higher education: Intergroup dialogue as pedagogy across the curriculum. *Multicultural Education, 21*(3), 51-61.

Clover, D. E., & Stalker, J. (2007). (Eds.). *The arts and social justice: Re-crafting adult education and community cultural leadership.* Gosport, UK: Ashford Colour Press.

Cole, A., & Knowles, J. G. (2000). *Researching teaching: Exploring teacher development through reflexive inquiry.* Boston: Allyn and Bacon.

Cole, A., & Knowles, J. G. (2008). Arts-informed research. In A. Cole & J. G. Knowles (Eds.), *Handbook of the arts in qualitative research: Perspectives, methodologies, examples, and issues* (pp. 55-70). Thousand Oaks, CA: Sage.

Coover, V., Deacon, E., Esser, C., & Moore, C. (1977). *Resource manual for a living revolution.* British Columbia: New Society.

Cunningham, B. (2002). *Mandala: Journey to the center.* New York: DK.

Darts, D. (2004). Visual culture jam: Art, pedagogy, and creative resistance. *Studies in Art Education, 45*(4), 313-327.

Day, C. (2002). Teachers' life worlds, agency, and policy contexts. *Teachers and Teaching: Theory and Practice, 8*(3/4), 421-434.

Day, L. (2002). "Putting yourself in other people's shoes": The use of forum theatre to explore refugee and homeless issues in schools. *Journal of Moral Education, 31*(1), 21-34.

DeCantias, C. (1996). What does drawing my hand have to do with leadership? A look at the process of leaders becoming artists. *Journal of Aesthetic Education, 30*(4), 87-97.

Dewey, J. (1934). *Art as experience.* New York: The Berkley Publishing Group.

Dissanayake, E. (1990). *What is art for?* Seattle: University of Washington Press.

Dissanayake, E. (1992). *Homo aestheticus: Where art comes from and why.* Seattle: University of Washington Press.

Dissanayake, E. (2000). *Art and intimacy: How the arts began.* Seattle: University of Washington Press.

Dutton, D. (1994). The experience of art is paradise regained: Kant on free and dependent beauty. *The British Journal of Aesthetics, 34*, 226-41.

Dutton, D. (2009). *The art instinct: Beauty, pleasure, and human evolution.* New York: Bloomsbury Press.

Eco, U. (2000). *Art and beauty in the middle ages.* New Haven, CT: Yale University Press.

Eisner, E. (1991). *The enlightened eye: Qualitative inquiry and the enhancement of educational practice.* New York: Macmillan.

Eisner, E. (2002a). *The arts and the creation of mind.* New Haven, CT: Yale University Press.

Eisner, E. (2002b). What can education learn from the arts about the practice of education? *Journal of Curriculum and Supervision, 18*(1), 4-16.

Eisner, E. (2008). Art and knowledge. In J. G. Knowles & A. L. Cole (Eds.), *Handbook of the arts in qualitative research* (pp. 3-12). Los Angeles: Sage.

Elstad, E. (2008). Towards a theory of mutual dependency between school administrators and teachers. *Education Management Administration & Leadership, 36*(3), 393-414.

Erdman, D. V. (Ed.). (1997). *The complete poetry & prose of William Blake.* New York: Anchor.

Fonseca, I. (1995). *Bury me standing: The Gypsies and their journey.* Vintage Brooks, NY: Random House.

Fontana, D. (2005). *Meditation with mandalas: 52 new mandalas to help you grow in peace and awareness.* London: Duncan Baird.

Foster, R., & St. Hilaire, B. (2004). The who, how, why, and what of leadership in secondary school improvement lessons learned in England. *Alberta Journal of Educational Research, 50*(44), 354-369.

Freire, P. (1972). *Pedagogy of the oppressed.* New York: Herder and Hearder.

Gadamer, H. G., Weinsheimer, J., & Marshall, D. G. (2004). *Truth and method* (2nd ed.). New York: Continuum.

Gardner, H. (1995). *Leading minds: An anatomy of leadership.* New York: Basic Books Harper Collins.

Geertz, C. (1983). *Local knowledge.* New York: Basic Books.

Giroux, H. (2001). *Theory and resistance in education: Towards a pedagogy for the opposition.* Westport, CT: Bergin & Garvey.

Giroux, H. (2006). Higher education under siege: Implications for public intellectuals. *NEA Higher Education Journal, 22,* 63-78.

235

Giroux, H., & Giroux, S. (2004). *Take back higher education: Race, youth, and the crisis of democracy in the post-civil rights era*. New York: Palgrave Macmillan.

Gladwell, M. (2002). *The tipping point*. Baltimore, MD: Back Bay.

Goodson, I., & Numan U. (2002). Teacher's life worlds, agency, and policy contexts. *Teachers and Teaching: Theory and Practice, 8*(3/4), 269-277.

Greene, M. (1979). Teaching: The question of personal reality. In A. Lieberman & L. Miller (Eds.), *Staff development: New demands, new realities, new perspectives* (pp. 23-25). New York: Teachers College Press.

Greene, M. (1995). *Releasing the imagination: Essays on education, the arts, and social change*. San Francisco: Jossey-Bass.

Greene, M. (2007a). *Imagination and becoming: Bronx charter school of the arts*. Retrieved February 3, 2009, from http://www.maxinegreene.org/articles.php

Greene, M. (2007b). *Countering indifference: The role of the arts*. Retrieved February 3, 2009, from http://www.maxinegreene.org/articles.php

Greene, M. (2007c). *Imagination and the healing arts*. Retrieved February 3, 2009, from http://www.maxinegreene.org/articles.php

Greene, M. (2007d). *Imagination, oppression, and culture/creating authentic openings*. Retrieved February 3, 2009, from http://www.maxinegreene.org/articles.php

Greene, M. (2007e). *Toward a pedagogy of thought and a pedagogy of imagination*. Retrieved February 3, 2009, from http://www.maxinegreene.org/articles.php

Greene, M. (2007f). *Counter indifference: The role of the arts*. Retrieved February 3, 2009, from http://www.maxinegreene.org/articles.php

Greene, M. (2007g). *Aesthetics as research*. Retrieved February 3, 2009, from http://www.maxinegreene.org/articles.php

Greene, M. (2007h). *In search of pedagogy*. Retrieved February 3, 2009, from http://www.maxinegreene.org/articles.php

Hamzeh, Z. (Director/Writer). (2003). *The letter: An American town and "the Somali invasion"* [Documentary film]. United States: Hamzeh Mystique Films.

Hansen, H., Ropo, A., & Sauer, E. (2007). Aesthetic leadership. *The Leadership Quarterly, 18*, 544-560.

Hatton, E. (1998). Writing and teaching about the oppressive 'isms' in teacher education: Taking a new direction through alternate forms of data representation. *Asia-Pacific Journal of Teacher Education, 26*(3), 217-234.

Heifetz, R. A. (1994). *Leadership without easy answers*. Cambridge, MA: The Belknap Press of Harvard University Press.

Heifetz, R. A., & Linsky, M. (2002). *Leadership on the line: Staying alive through the dangers of leading*. Boston: Harvard Business School Press.

Humphreys, M., Brown, A., & Hatch, M. J. (2003). Is enthography jazz? *Organization, 10*(1), 5-13.

Johnson, L. (2002). Art-centered approaches to diversity education in teaching and learning. *Multicultural Education, 9*(4), 18-21.

Jung, C. G. (1964) *Man and his symbols*. Garden City, NY: DoubleDay.

Katz, S., & Ryan, D. (2005). Two women professors search for tools to teach social justice. *Advancing Women, 18.* Retrieved February 3, 2009, from http://www.advancingwomen.com/

Keats, J. (1819). *Ode on a Grecian urn*. Retrieved February 3, 2009, from http://www.bartleby.com/101/625.html

Kelly, R., & Leggo, C. (2008) *Creative expression, creative education: Creativity as a primary rationale for education*. Calgary, Canada: Detselig Enterprises.

Kenny, C. B. (1982). *The mythic artery: The magic of music therapy*. Alascadero, CA: Ridgeview.

Kenny, C. B. (1989). *The field of play: A guide for the theory and practice of music therapy*. Alascadero, CA: Ridgeview.

Kenny, C. B. (1998). A sense of art: A First Nations view. *Canadian Journal of Native Education, 22*(1), 77-84.

Kenny, C. B. (2006). *Music & life in the field of play: An anthology*. Gilsum, NH: Barcelona.

Knipe, M. (2004). Passport to understanding. *Arts & Activities, 134*(5), 24-25.

LaBoskey, V. K. (2006). "Reality check": Teachers' lives as policy critique. *Teachers and Teaching: Theory and Practice, 12*(2), 111-122.

Ladkin, D. (2008). Leading beautifully: How mastery, congruence, and purpose create the aesthetic of embodied leadership practice. *The Leadership Quarterly, 19,* 31-41.

Lattimer, H. (2007). To help and not hinder. *Educational Leadership, 65*(1), 70-73.

Leggo, C. (2004) Tangled lines: On autobiography and poetic knowing. In A. Cole, L. Neilsen, J. G. Knowles, & T. Luciani (Eds.). *Provoked by art: Theorizing arts-informed research* (pp. 18-35). Alberta, Canada: Backalong Books.

Lynn, M., & Smith, M. R. (2007). Preservice teacher inquiry: Creating a space to
dialogue about becoming a social justice educator. *Teaching and Teacher
Education, 23*(1), 94-105.

Luciani, T. (2004). From the heart: Fragments, family, roots and listening. In A. Cole,
L. Neilsen, J. G. Knowles, & T. Luciani (Eds.). *Provoked by art: Theorizing
arts-informed research* (pp. 36-43). Alberta, Canada: Backalong Books.

Mandela, N. (1994). Quotation from inaugural speech.
Retrieved February 3, 2009, from
http://thinkexist.com/quotation/as_we_are_liberated_from_our_own_fearour/14
4636.htl

Maxcy, S. J. (1995). *Democracy, chaos, and the new school order*. Thousand Oaks,
CA: Sage.

McGhan, B. (2002). A fundamental education reform: Teacher-led schools. *Phi Delta
Kappan, 83*(7), 3.

McNiff, S. (1992). *Art as medicine: Creating a therapy of the imagination*. Boston:
Shambhala.

McNiff, S. (1998). *Art-based research*. London: Jessica Kinglsey.

Mizanoglu, M. (1998). *Persona: The meaning behind the mask*. Northampton, MA:
BGB Press.

Neilsen, L. (2004). Aesthetics and knowing: Ephemeral principles for a groundless
theory. In A. Cole, L. Neilsen, J. G. Knowles, & T. Luciani (Eds.). *Provoked by
art: Theorizing arts-informed research* (pp. 52-61). Alberta, Canada: Backalong
Books.

Noel, J. R. (2003). Creating artwork in response to issues of social justice: A critical
multicultural pedagogy. *Multicultural Education, 10*(4), 15-18.

Palmer, P. (1998). *The courage to teach: Exploring the inner landscape of a teacher's
life*. San Francisco, CA: Jossey-Bass.

Pinar, W. F. (1994). *Autobiography, politics and sexuality: Essays in curriculum
theory 1972-1992*. New York: Peter Lang.

Rapp, D. (2002). Social justice and the importance of rebellious, oppositional
imaginations. *Journal of School Leadership, 12*, 226-245.

Read, H. (1965). *Icon & idea: The function of art in the development of human
consciousness*. New York: Harvard University Press.

Rhodes, C. (2000). *Outsider art: Spontaneous alternatives (world of art)*. London: Thames & Hudson.

Rhyne, J. (1996). *The gestalt art experience: Patterns that connect.* Chicago: Magnolia Street.

Richards, M. C. (1989). *Centering: In pottery, poetry, and the person.* Middletown, CT: Wesleyan University Press.

Roberts, R. A., Bell, L., & Murphy, B. (2008). Flipping the script: Analyzing youth talk about race and racism. *Anthropology and Education Quarterly, 29*(3), 334-354.

Rodgers, C. R. (2006). "The truning of one's soul"—Learning to teach for social justice: The Putney graduate school of teacher education (1950-1964). *Teachers College Record, 108*(0), 1266-1295.

Rogers, C. (1980). *A way of being.* New York: Houghton Mifflin.

Rogers, N. (1993). *The creative connection: Expressive arts as healing.* Palo Alto, CA: Science and Behavior Books.

Ross, J., Bradley Cousins, J., Gadalla, T., & Hannay, L. (1999). Administrative assignment of teachers in restructuring secondary schools: The effect of out-of-field course responsibility on teacher efficacy. *Educational Administration Quarterly, 35*(5), 782-805.

Rowley, J. (1988). The teacher as leader and teacher educator. *Journal of Teacher Education, 29*(3), 13-16.

Runco, M. A. (2007) Creativity theories and themes: Research, development, and practice. San Diego, CA: Academic Press.

Scarry, E. (1999). *On beauty and being just.* Princeton: University Press.

Schon, D. (1987). *Educating the reflective pracitioner.* San Francisco: Jossey-Bass.

Schneidewind, N., & Davidson, E. (2006). *Open minds to equality: A sourcebook of learning activities to affirm diversity and promote equity* (3rd ed.). Milwaukee, WI: Rethinking Schools.

Schwandt, T. (1997). *Qualitative inquiry: A dictionary of terms.* Thousand Oaks, CA: Sage.

Senge, P. (1990). *The fifth discipline: The art and practice of the learning organization.* New York: Bantam Doubleday Dell.

Shor, I. (1980). (Ed.). *Critical teaching and everyday life.* Montreal: Black Rose Books.

Shapiro, L. (2004). *Disrupting what is going on: Women educational leaders make art together to transform themselves and their schools.* Unpublished doctoral dissertation, Union Institute and University, Cincinnati, OH.

Shapiro, L. (2006). Releasing emotion: Artmaking and leadership for social justice. In C. Marshall & M. Oliva (Eds.), *Leadership for social justice: Making revolutions in education* (pp. 233-250). Boston: Pearson.

Spalding, E., & Wilson, A. (2002). Demystifying reflection: A study of pedagogical strategies that encourage reflective journaling writing. *Teachers College Record, 104*(7), 1393-1421.

Sternberg, R. J. (1999). *Handbook of creativity.* New York: Cambridge University Press.

Sternberg, R. J., Grigorenko, E. L., & Singer, J. L. (2004). *Creativity: From potential to realization.* Washington, DC: American Psychological Association.

Suominen, A. (2006). Writing with photographs writing self: Using artistic methods in the investigation of identity. *International Journal of Education Through Art, 2*(2), 139-156.

Thomas, S. (2004). Art-making and theorizing through the language of imagery. In A. Cole, L. Neilsen, J. G. Knowles, & T. Luciani (Eds.). *Provoked by art: Theorizing arts-informed research* (pp. 62-70). Alberta, Canada: Backalong Books.

Togut, S. (2004). *Mandala.* Unpublished Handout.

Tyack, D., & Cuban, L. (1995). *Tinkering toward utopia: A century of public school reform.* Cambridge, MA: Harvard University Press.

Urbanski, A., & Nickolaou, M. B. (1997). Reflections on teachers as leaders. *Educational Policy,* 11(2), 243.

Vaill, P. B. (1989). *Managing as a performing art: New ideas for a world of chaotic change.* San Francisco: Jossey-Bass.

Valli, L. (1997). Listening to other voices: A description of teacher reflection in the United States. *Peabody Journal of Education, 72*(1), 67-88.

Van Manen, M. (1990). *Researching lived experience: Human science for an action sensitive pedagogy.* Albany, NY: State University Press.

Wilson, E. O. (1978). *On Human Nature.* Cambridge, MA: Harvard University Press.

Wilson, E. O. (1984). *Biophilia.* Cambridge: Harvard University Press.

Witherspoon, G. (1977). *Language and art in the Navajo universe*. Ann Arbor, MI: University Press.

Young, I. (1990). *Justice and the politics of difference*. Princeton, NJ: University Press.

Made in the USA
Lexington, KY
22 June 2013